Courage, Confidence and Competence

Essays on Stupidity and Decline

Pearce Deacon

https://pearcedeacon.wordpress.com/

Table of Contents

Introduction..1

Courage, Confidence & Competence...............................2

Why are People Stupid?...8

Innovation, degradation, and delusion.........................13

Change is not always good..17

Respect..20

Those Pesky Words Keep Getting in the Way!.................23

It's a Dog's Life..29

Is the USA still a Constitutional Republic....................37

Stoicism in a Nutshell..41

Stoicism: Negative Visualization vs Negative Attitude......44

A Letter...47

Freedom vs Freedom...51

How to Get Rich!...55

Decency...59

How to be a Lying Turd...62

The Lesson of Lot's Wife — Its not about sex................65

Another European Dark Age, or the Beginning of a Fourth Renaissance?
....68

On Having a Credo..74

Why be a Prepper?..77

Radical Islam is not caused by Socio-Economic Injustice.....80

Islam is NOT a Backwards Religion..............................89

Thoughts after 2 years an expat in Tbilisi, Georgia — Mostly sadness. .95

The Dangerous Emergence of "Protester Culture".............100

The Difference Between Error and Evil..........................104

The Origins of Israel: British Colonialism, Zionism, or Arab Stupidity
....110

A Discouraging Afternoon in Old Town Vienna............................118
A response to a proposition regarding Basic Jobs vs Basic Income......120
What is the democratization process?......................................126
Love vs Utility...129
The Failure of Modern Western Democracy..........................135
The Five Stages of Grief...139
The Ideologies of ANTIFA and BLM in a Nutshell...............143
A response to a video from Russel Brand..............................147
Long Live the Revolution!..150
The Psychology of Freedom… or Not Giving a Shit?............155

Introduction

This is a collection of essays I have written over the years that are only related by the underlying subject matter of stupidity and social decline. Most of the essays deal in some way with stupidity, whether to describe or evaluate these issues, or try to counteract them.

I hope you enjoy!

Courage, Confidence & Competence

My friends and I have been debating why our favorite franchises have been turning to crap. That is entertainment franchises like Star Trek, Star Wars, Doctor Who, etc., not fast food franchises. The accepted answer to this is: Go Woke Go Broke!

That is rather convenient, and there is enough truth to be convincing… yet I am not convinced. Hollyweird was woke before 'woke' was a word. In the old days they were not woke, they were good old fashioned 'commie pinko faggots' (hey, that's what they were called – don't shoot the messenger snowflake)! And that was fine! Because regardless of what you called them, they made damned good movies and TV shows. Who cared about their ideology, gender identification, alphabet code, or pronouns? I didn't.

The difference between yesterday's Hollyweirdos and today's Hollyweirdos has to do with competence. The old Hollyweirdos were competent. Today's Hollyweirdos are incompetent… and they know it. So they hide behind being 'woke' like a shield. And so far it has been working for them. If you don't like the crap they are producing you are an *ist or a *phobe of some sort.

If this was limited to Hollyweird I would not care, but it is not. Our government is filled with the worst 'woke' incompetents who use the same tactics, as is our military, our education system, Big Business, and every other aspect of our society! If they were woke and competent I don't think most people would care that much. The problem is they are not competent, they know they are not competent, and their self-defense mechanism is to attack those who complain about their incompetence as 'istaphobes'. It becomes a matter of power rather than ideology or taste. And those in power today are the most incompetent.

*****

I look around at the world today, and more particularly the United States of America, and I am filled with a mixture shame, horror, and dread. We are living in a world of cowards lead by fools.

What happened to all those dreams of progress of the 20th Century?

There are usually two types of answers to such a historical question: one that is specific and one that is hopelessly vague.

For instance, "What happened to Anglo-Saxon Britain?" This question can be answered with an answer that is more or less correct if a bit oversimplified: In 1066 William the Conqueror, Duke of Normandy, invaded England and defeated the forces of Harold Godwinson, King of the England and the Danelaw, at the Battle of Hastings. With that defeat came the end of Anglo-Saxon Britain, and the beginning of Norman Britain. There is a lot more to it than that, but I think most historians would acknowledge, even if with some discomfort and resentment, that this simple answer is more or less correct.

Other questions cannot be answered so simply: "What happened to the Ottoman Empire?" This question cannot be glibly answered with a date and a brief reference to a small battle. The collapse of the Ottoman Empire was a slow and confusing process. From the grandeur created after the capture of Constantinople in 1453, there was a slow decline interrupted from time to time with sparks of brilliance, expansion, and glory. There are a lot of theories, some more complex and nuanced than others, but none of them are simple.

In trying to understand what is happening here and now in the 21st Century, or perhaps more distressing what has already happened, to the United States in particular and the West in general, I believe it is going to be more like the second question. There is no single event that can explain why the West is failing, or has already failed. But I will lay out my current theory: Generational Degeneracy.

*****

I am in a rather odd situation; I am part of Generation-X, but my parents were part of the Greatest Generation. The parents of my friends growing up were all Baby-Boomers who had a very different attitude about things. My parents survived the Great Depression and my father fought in World War II. The parents of my friends danced to Chuck Berry, and worshiped the memory of John F. Kennedy. I look at my generation, Generation-X, with disgust; they are nothing more than a bunch weak degenerate losers. My fellow Generation-X members think they are the greatest thing since sliced bread.

What does all this mean – the Greatest Generation, Baby-Boomers, and Generation-X? My personal experiences and studies suggest that our society has been in a steady decline since the rise of the Greatest Generation to the present. The Greatest Generation was made up of people who were educated in the school of hard knocks; really hard knocks – the Great Depression and World War II. They learned from painful reality that some things worked, some things did not work, and that if you got it wrong you were going to suffer. Yet despite the Greatest Generation being some of the most profoundly conservative of people due to the hardships they suffered yet survived, they were also more innovative and willing to take risks than those who came before them and the worthless generation they spawned – the Baby-Boomers. In the end, we must conclude that the Greatest Generation had courage, confidence, and competence. This made it possible for them to overcome immense obstacles without becoming bitter, vindictive, or entitled.

Despite the many successes of the Greatest Generation, it had a great failure: they failed to raise the next generation to have those same traits that served them so well. Where the Greatest Generation had courage, the Baby-Boomers were cowards. It is said that courage is the most important virtue since without it the other virtues are meaningless. The Baby-Boomers had confidence and competence, but without courage it was all meaningless. Ultimately the Baby-Boomers fit perfectly into the hollow-man model described by C.S. Lewis in his essay, 'Men Without Chests'. For Lewis, people without 'chests' are people that lack the connection between mind and body, thought and morality, intelligence and wisdom. As Lewis stated, "We make men without chests and expect from them virtue and enterprise… We laugh at honor and are shocked to find traitors in our midst." The Baby-Boomers were raised by the Greatest Generation yet rejected all of the fine character traits that made them Great. Instead, the Baby-Boomers were technicians who thought they did not need courage, nor honor, nor integrity. They could fiddle with a dial here, select the appropriate button there, and everything would be fine.

And for the Baby-Boomers it was all fine. Because of the inheritance of achievement the Greatest Generation left to them the Baby-Boomers were able to skip along without much challenge. But even the Baby-Boomers recognized that they were not leaving the same world for their children that had been left for them. The Baby-Boomers knowingly handed to their children a soiled legacy; a degenerate prosperity. And they taught Generation-X to believe they had a right to everything in the universe without the need to earn it. It would just fall in their lap.

And again, it did. Generation-X was born into a prosperity that prior generations would have considered quite impossible. Like their parents they lacked courage, but sadly they also lacked the competence of the Baby-Boomers. For Generation-X everything was a game which they were confident they would win – even if they lacked the skill to complete the simplest of tasks. They were Confident; not because they were better, smarter, or tried harder, but because they deserved it! They rose in the corporate hierarchies by cutting down those before them, accomplishing nothing of use or benefit for anyone. Generation-X was good at nothing more than filling their bellies and stuffing their wallets. The world was their oyster, and they sucked it dry leaving a dry shriveled husk for those that followed.

The children of Generation-X, the Millennials, came into a world that was filled with a strange mix of fools, ne'er-do-wells, and the hopelessly despondent. They were raised in houses more sumptuous than the greatest aristocrats of previous ages could have imagined, yet they wallow in ghetto style degradation worshiping degenerate pseudo-gangsters, pimps and whores. They receive better food and healthcare than the wealthiest of the Robber Barons of the 19th Century could have expected, and yet they are fat, pallid, weak, and dependent upon drugs. Their toys are more complex and riveting than the tools of their forefathers, but they build nothing that is real or tangible. The Millennials lack for nothing… and they value and appreciate nothing. They have everything except courage, confidence, and competence. Instead they cultivate a sense of grievance.

*****

And here we are trapped in the 21st Century surrounded by people without virtue, modesty, intelligence, wisdom, or any concept of consequence. We have foolishly spent our inheritance on shiny baubles, worthless trifles, and depraved entertainment, and we have left the world worse than we found it.

Why are People Stupid?

I often ask myself this question. I am really curious. Perhaps the better question is, "Why do people do stupid things?"

There is one answer that comes immediately to mind:

People do stupid things because they are stupid!

Not only does this seem obvious, but it is also very satisfying to call someone stupid when they disagree with me. After all, what other possible reason could anyone have to disagree with me????

However, no matter how satisfying it may be to write off my detractors as being stupid, even if it is true, it does not explain the bigger picture. Most people who do stupid things are not stupid (even when they disagree with me). They are often very smart at many things.

Although I have not done a scientific study on this, I have not obtained a PhD on the subject, nor have I read a scientific study by someone else with a PHD, I think it is fair to say that smart people do stupid things just as much as not-so-smart people. If anything smart people do stupid things more often.

Why?

You would think that having a higher intellect would protect smart people somewhat?

There are many types of "intelligence".

The somewhat new theory of 'Multiple Intelligence' breaks down the classical view of intelligence into 9 classes: Naturalistic, Musical, Logical-Mathematical, Existential, Interpersonal, Bodily-Kinesthetic, Linguistic, Intra-Personal, and Spatial. Some may not be very good at math but they may be very good at one or more of the other 8, and to limit the measure of intelligence to math is unfair, inaccurate, and detrimental to the understanding of human existence.

I have always found this to be very interesting, and I believe it is true. But in my opinion there is another simpler way of classifying intelligence:

Intellectual, Emotional, and Wisdom.

In regards to Intellectual, I will go ahead and concede that the above 9 types of intelligence can and should be included. This type of intelligence is the measure of how we accomplish the day to day tasks in our lives, and how we respond to things that happen to us.

Emotional intelligence deals with our ability to manage our emotions and the emotions of others. It is broken down into 3 parts: 1. emotional awareness or empathy, 2. the ability to use your emotions productively, and 3. the ability to manage emotions — yours and others — in other words maturity and leadership.

A lot of studies over the years (perhaps centuries) have been done on intellectual and emotional intelligence even if not always in those words. But the ancient and venerated study of

Wisdom seems to have been abandoned. Who needs Wisdom when you can do some or all those 9 wonderful things described under Multiple Intelligence? Our education system and society is entirely focused on getting you to pursue those sorts of intelligence. When things don't quite work out emotional intelligence is examined as a possible cure. Wisdom? Who needs it?!

Wisdom has been defined in many ways: "The quality or state of being wise; knowledge of what is true or right coupled with just judgment as to action; sagacity, discernment, or insight." (dictionary.com). Wikipedia suggests that Wisdom is the ability to think and act using knowledge, experience, understanding, common sense, and insight. I suppose another way of trying to understand something is to look at its opposite: Foolishness. Wisdom is the ability to discern between what is Wise and what is Foolish.

I never really liked the 20th Century. Everything seemed to move too fast in some ways, and too slow in others. Flight and train schedules seemed to determine everything, thinking about why you are going somewhere not so important. However, the 21st Century has left me even more profoundly disappointed. The 21st Century has become the Century of Foolishness. People around the globe are encouraged to study, work hard, focus on this or that, become GREAT at something, push hard, dream big, think positive, don't give up, move ahead, etc. etc. etc.

That does not leave a lot of time for thoughts like:

- Why am I here?

- What is the meaning of life?

- What is really important?

- What is the difference between happiness and satisfaction?

- What does it mean to be ethical and why should I care?

- What is the difference between right and wrong?

I could go on.

But I won't. People don't care about any of those things. Why bother when you dream of driving a new car, or living in a new house, or getting a new phone, etc. None of those question are going to help you get any of that!

So instead we learn how to build better devices and to sell them to others in interesting and alluring ways all without thinking about why we are doing anything. That is stupid if you ask me.

So why do smart people do stupid things? They may be the best doctors, lawyers, athletes, engineers, entertainers, businessmen, etc., and they may have empathy and maturity by the bucket load, but they have no Wisdom. They are Fools.

Where can you find Wisdom? Its all around you, but you have to stop what you are doing long enough to see. The ancient world was full of Wisdom (and I suppose also Foolishness). Most religions and philosophies focus a great deal on teaching Wisdom instead of how to build houses, bows and arrows, spears, and chariots, or how to succeed in business or conquest. Put down the tools of your trade, and find time to pick up a book. I believe the Bible is full of useful information about how to be Wise. The guys who wrote the Bible may not be very helpful when it comes to fixing your car, or getting your laptop working, but they knew a lot about people. And without radio, TV, or Internet they had a lot of time to think about things. I personally find the teachings of the ancient and modern Stoics to be very helpful.

Ultimately if you want to be Wise you are going to have to think a great deal about Wisdom and Foolishness. That is what Wisdom is all about; knowing the difference.

I suppose the real secret to being Wise is this: You have to want to be Wise.

Innovation, degradation, and delusion

"People who create things nowadays can expect to be prosecuted by highly moralistic people who are incapable of creating anything. There is no way to measure the chilling effect on innovation that results from the threats of taxation, regulation and prosecution against anything that succeeds. We'll never know how many ideas our government has aborted in the name protecting us."
— *Joseph Sobran*

"Revolutionary" is a term bandied about today to describe just about everything except for those things which are really novel and innovative. However, when one looks at the 100 year period from 1890 to 1990 I think it is fair to describe the innovations developed during that period as revolutionary. In every aspect of human activity progress advanced at a breathtaking pace, and America led the way.

What has happened since 1990? There has been a tremendous amount of innovation in the world, but little of it has come from America. As Mark Steyn points out we have spent billions of dollars on medical research, and the only condition we have been able to cure is erectile dysfunction. And even that was an accident. The scientists were actually diligently researching the ever important issue of balding and discovered an interesting side effect. We have also abandoned our leadership in every other aspect of scientific research intended to better the human condition. We have given up on curing diseases, and instead focus on how to keep people from getting fat, depressed, or anxious (at best). We no longer try to develop new and affordable means of transportation like high-speed rail, supersonic jets, etc. The space race is now a distant memory for us; no research platforms located in geosynchronous orbit for us. All those pursuits and many more have been picked up by our competitors around the world while America languishes in Reality TV oblivion.

There are a few industries we still seem to dominate: internet pornography. We have surpassed the Swedes in this vital area of human behavior with California becoming a global center of production. Who needs scientific innovation when you can have a steady stream of free pornography and cheap designer drugs to satisfy, or perhaps deaden, your every desire.

Although America has accomplished little during the last 30 years Americans have learned to be extremely confident in our lack of accomplishments. I think it is fair to say Americans have become the most successful people in promoting self-esteem. I remember reading a study about global math skills; needless to say American students performed poorly. The interesting aspect of the study was the student attitudes in regards to their abilities. Before and after the test American students believed they had performed much better than they had actually scored. Asian students on the other hand, who had in fact performed much better, believed their personal performance was far worse. I can only suspect the Japanese students must have been suicidal after the test.

So much for self-esteem. Without real accomplishment self-esteem does very little.

And that is where we come to delusion. It appears if you feed self-esteem to people long enough they become truly insane. Just look at the entire nation of Greece. A few years ago there was a study asking all Europeans who are the hardest working people in Europe. Clearly the Germans won, and quite justifiably. It was a conclusion that few contested. The French are quite proud of their culture but they are wise enough to know that they are not the hardest working. The same can be said for Spain and Italy. They did not fool themselves into believing that hard work was part of their national character. But not so for the Greeks who when polled believed that they were the hardest working people in Europe. Now I love Greece and I love the Greeks, but no rational person after spending any amount of time in the country would conclude that the Greeks suffer from working too hard. In fact I would have to say that they may very well be the laziest group of people in Europe, which is just fine by me. It is perhaps one of the things that is most charming about Greece; a decidedly slower pace to things. However the Greeks seem to have mastered the power of self-esteem to the point of insane delusion. I think the last election in Greece confirms this. They confidently voted themselves into prosperity; who needs hard work, a responsible government, or a competitive business environment?

As an American I see my country going the same path. We have abandoned innovation, embraced degradation, and are on the path to complete and total delusion. We are not quite as desperately insane as the Greeks, who have nothing whatsoever to support their delusions of grandeur (after all WE can still bomb the begeezus out of just about anyone in the world), but we are on our way.

Change is not always good

One of the most damaging concepts of the modern age is that change is always good. This is a profound and dangerous fallacy.

To understand why this is the case let us begin with the primary law of the universe. Entropy.

> *Entropy holds that everything interferes with everything else. In the process everything slows down. And as things slow down things break. And as things break they disintegrate into nothingness. Things decay.*

Thus it is the fundamental law of the universe that things disintegrate into nothingness. Rather depressing really. Many artists, poets, and songwriters have commented on how pointless it is to struggle against entropy. I recall a rather depressing Pink Floyd song about this very issue.

However there seems to be some exceptions to this rule of universal decay. Some things defy entropy and keep other things together. Life is an example of entropy-defying order. Generation after generation, life continues and actually seems to improve. At least if you consider things becoming more complex, more ordered, and more functional as improvements.

Complexity requires order to continue, and order is the opposite of decay.

So what does entropy have to do with whether or not change is always good?

If something exists it is evidence that it is working—it is defying entropy and decay. If something can defy decay it is evidence that there is something maintaining the order. We may not know and understand what is opposing entropy and decay, but it is would seem to be doing its job at promoting order and preserving complexity.

With that in mind 'change for the sake of change' is insanity. Suicidal even. Changing things that work is not a good idea unless you are improving upon the process; that is increasing the decay-defying order.

Take for example a car. For a car to function thousands of different pieces must perfectly fit together and work in harmony. *(I think it is worth pointing out, even if a bit off point, that this car did not assemble itself. It was designed to work. It was built by others. But even if it did somehow assemble itself over time it functions because of a complex set of systems that work together. Take out a key part and the entire system fails. So if you believe that the order you find in the universe is created or evolved, it is the order that keeps things working. Remove that order and you see chaos and decay.)* Perhaps it is possible to improve upon how a car functions, and such change would be useful and welcome. However just taking parts out of a working automobile without understanding how the parts work together and without understanding the consequences of removing those parts will result in disaster. The car will cease to function, it will decay, and eventually disappear. That is bad.

Unless of course your goal is to destroy the car.

The undeniable nature of the universe is decay. The fact that some things exist is evidence that those things work at defying decay, at maintaining order. The very existence of something over time is a profound fact that should be considered very carefully. Perhaps even admired and respected. Changing the nature of a thing may destroy the order that is resisting decay, and maintaining complexity. Change therefore is not always good.

Unless you believe that chaos and decay are good. Blindly changing things that work will most likely result in those things breaking. And things that break in this universe disappear, and turn to nothing.

If you admire existence you will seek decay-defying order and will view change with caution, perhaps even distrust. If you admire nothing, or perhaps nothingness, you will seek the chaos of constant change.

Respect

I was thinking about how to respond to a particular acquaintance who is always trying to convince me that I need to expand my 'brand' through some flaky form of marketing. What is odd is that I am much more successful, prosperous, and satisfied than he is. However, he is the one always trying to educate me on the importance of promoting myself to others. I realize he is never going to listen to anything I say, so I decided to write this down instead.

There are three rules (or perhaps more accurately personal traits) that I find help me to be more prosperous and satisfied.

1. I don't really care what people think of me. Don't get me wrong, sometimes I am troubled when people misunderstand me or have a low opinion of me, but when push comes to shove I don't really care what they think. At least not enough to let it trouble me. I don't understand why this is the case since it is so contrary to how other people think and feel. All I know is at about the age of 12 to 13 I began to have less and less interest in what others thought of me with the sole exception being the opinions of those for whom I had a profound respect. I am much older now and that process has only increased as I age. As I look back I have many regrets for things I have done and things that I have failed to do, but I have no regret regarding

my lack of interest in what others think of me. Putting a high value on things that are worthless is foolishness.

2. I do not automatically have respect for others. I suppose this rule is somewhat related to Number 1, but I do not have very much respect for people until they prove to me that they deserve my respect. This does not mean that I treat people with disrespect, only that within my mind most people do not impress me in any particular way. I try to treat everyone with the same respect that I would like to be treated, but that is the extent of my respect. If you want my respect you have to earn it, and most do not even make the attempt.

3. Finally, I demand respect from those that I associate with, at least to the limited extent that I can enforce such a demand. I do not bluster about how people should treat me. I simply refuse to voluntarily interact with people who do not show me the proper level of respect. I do not happily tolerate anyone laying hands upon me, insulting me, or treating me with contempt and disregard. Treating me in such a manner may not result in a violent response on my part, but it will result in my withdrawing from any further interaction or contact with the offending parties. I prefer my own company over bad company, and I will not associate with people in business or in my personal life who fail to treat me properly. I suppose this is also related to the issue of trust. Once someone has lost my trust it is very difficult to regain it.

These three rules have served me well. In business I refuse to associate with people who lack integrity, and who do not value what I have to offer. Instead I focus upon providing the very best I can offer to those who do value me, and charging an appropriately higher amount for those services. I discovered very early in my business that I should 'fire' clients who show me disrespect in any way, particularly those who fail to pay me the agreed upon sum for my services. I cannot look back with regret upon a single case where I ended a business relationship that was turning bad or annoying to me. Quite the opposite is true; I regret not terminating relationships earlier. As a result I spend my time productively working for honest and respectful clients who view me as a valuable resource.

Similarly in my personal life I refuse to interact with people who treat me with disrespect or who I do not respect. As a result I don't have a lot of friends, but I highly value those that I have. Wasting time on people who do not deserve your respect or who do not give you respect is the height of folly. I have never regretted having high standards or in placing a very high value on myself.

Those Pesky Words Keep Getting in the Way!

One of the things that most irritates me about the Left is the historical habit of the Left to rob or distort the meanings of politically loaded words in an effort to disarm their political opponents. This intentional misuse of language is shown clearly in George Orwell's book "1984".

The most obvious examples of this is the hijacking of the terms "liberal" and "progressive". These terms were initially used in the late 18th Century and throughout the 19th Century to describe a political movement that supported the high ideals of the enlightenment. Such stellar figures as John Locke, Adam Smith, and John Stuart Mill are but a few of the intellectual giants that posited the notion that Man is a noble creature and that giving Man freedom, under proper conditions, will create a better society. The American Revolution was inspired by such thinkers, and Jefferson, Franklin and Madison are just a few political leaders that were described as Liberal. In fact, even those who politically opposed Jefferson in the United States were really not against Liberalism so much as in favor of different methods of pursuing those ideals.

The opposite of Liberals during this period were generally considered Conservatives, and they favored such wrong-headed beliefs as divine right, aristocratic privilege, and the backward economic theory of mercantilism.

In addition to Liberals and Conservatives, there was also a nascent movement later described as socialism, though it went under many names. Socialism and Liberalism were both products of the modern world, whereas Conservatives were trying to cling to a fast receding past, but the two modern movements had little in common other than a shared desire for change.

By the end of the 19th Century, the socialist movement had reached what it then perceived as a peak in Europe (perhaps even a plateau), and was becoming frustrated by a considerable opposition. Not only were the Conservatives opposed to the socialist movement, which openly promoted the stripping of property rights, and the removal of economic as well as political choice in society, but the Liberals and Progressives were also opposed to socialism on the basis that depriving men of their fundamental rights was against everything that they stood for, regardless of such issues as social inequality.

Instead of trying to reason with the opposition, or trying to convince the voters that socialism was a good thing, the clever socialist strategists of the day decided to simply "steal" the names and identities of the Liberal movements. Socialists began presenting themselves as Liberals, even though their credo was the exact opposite of the Liberal ideals. In addition, the socialists began pasting the term Conservative on anybody who opposed them, including the True Liberals.

When socialists were confronted with the inaccuracy of these descriptions, they simply yelled louder and declared anyone who opposed them to be out-dated Reactionaries. The True Liberals, sons of the Age of Enlightenment, were not intellectual street fighters, and unwittingly conceded the debate by shrugging it off as trivial and unimportant. Soon the term "Conservative" with all its negative connotations was being applied to people who believed in the noble nature of Man and the inalienable rights to life, liberty and the pursuit of happiness.

Because of the socialist manipulation of language, today we see a political spectrum that is simply inaccurate as well as misleading. We have the Left which is now defined as being Liberal, and we have the Right which is defined as Conservative. Lost is the important nuance of idealism and the role of the individual in regards to liberty and personal choice. This was exactly the goal of the 19th Century socialists.

Now idealists who believe in the fundamental rights of all humans to live free and without oppression have to share the political stage with strange archaic groups that often promote racism and hate. And the socialists who propose to deprive people of their individual liberties in exchange for a squalid inequality devoid of human free will and independence are defined as the Free Thinkers because there is no one else sitting next to them on the Left.

How did this strange schism among modern political movements take place?

We must look back to the 18th Century to find the cause for all this confusion and misunderstanding. As I described above, the Age of Enlightenment brought with it the novel and uplifting idea that Man was a noble creature, and that under the right circumstances he could create a fair and just society founded upon the ideals of freedom and personal choice. However, these ideas were not universally accepted, even among the "modernists" of the day. An example of this is a French philosopher named Jean Jacques Rousseau who believed that man had a solitary and savage nature, and that only in a rigidly coordinated society could man ever achieve his true higher calling. David Hume also shared many of these same view on the nature of man. This view is often referred to as the Naturalist Ideal due its self-purported goal of re-introducing mankind back into a "state of nature" that was passive and tranquil.

When we examine the major movements of the 18th Century, we see the American Revolution which was guided by the ideals of Liberalism, and we see that the French Revolution which was guided by the Naturalist views of Jean Jacques Rousseau. Under the American Revolution we witnessed the flowering of one of the greatest experiments in the history of man. Although not perfect, the American Revolution created a nation of laws and ideas where men were allowed to make their own choices regarding all manner of issues from where they could live, what profession they could choose, who would lead them, and even who they could marry. The French Revolution on the other hand was a dismal failure.

Whereas the American Revolution relied upon basic human nature properly channeled by a "self-interest well understood" and a small limited government to guide and direct the nature of the nation, the French Revolution saw Man as a small, weak, sordid, and evil thing that must be reshaped to fit into the grand visions of the intellectual followers and heirs of Rousseau. Soon the high ideals of the French Revolutionaries were being drowned in the blood of anyone who even seemed to oppose the grand strategy of the Revolution. Words were redefined, the calendar was changed, terms of endearment were frowned upon unless there was a patriotic purpose to them.

The effort to reshape Man from his limited existence into a grand social animal met with failure, and was eventually replaced by a profound tyranny that dogs Europe to this day. And the worst of it is that the supporters of this Naturalist view refused to go away quietly. Instead of looking at the profound success of the American Revolution and accepting that the views underlying the French Revolution were simply wrong, the Naturalists went from a basically optimistic view that although Man is a corrupt animal he can be improved upon, to a more cynical view that generally blamed the failures of the French Revolution upon its very victims. The People were simply not ready for the ennobling and enlightened views of the failed intellectuals. This strategy on how to deal with the unpleasant consequence of failure is something the modern socialists have been quick to adopt.

While the frustrated European intellectuals continued to reformat their failed ideals into what eventually took the shape of socialism, the American Revolution continued to grow and prosper. The inherent evil of slavery was finally abolished, and many of the inequalities that were inherited from the "ancient regime" were slowly yet steadily removed in what many have described as an evolutionary process, not a revolutionary one. By the end of the 19th Century it was hard for any honest person to review the facts and conclude anything other than that the ideals of the Liberal movement which were the basis of the American Revolution were a huge success, and as such should be promoted and emulated by societies and nations everywhere.

Yet a century later the True Liberal movement stands discredited virtually everywhere, suffering perhaps from an over-abundance of success, and the dark view of Rousseau and his socialists descendants now seem to rule supreme. Was it all because of the dishonest use of words by the Left? Or is there something else to explain this strange turn of events? Either way, we live in a world that could benefit from restoring the true meaning to words, and insisting that people remember that words have meaning and to stand by and allow unreasonable deviations can lead to disaster.

It's a Dog's Life

This morning I had a chat with a young girl who was complaining about being harassed by a neighbor's unruly dog. She said that the dog was not mean, but that it was playing with her a little more aggressively than she liked. I told her that she should have her family contact the owner of the dog and if that does not work contact the city. Her response was that the dog just needed a friend.

I paused for a moment, and then tried to explain to her that dogs do not need friends so much as they need structure and order that they can comprehend. She looked confused. I explained to her that in nature dogs form 'packs' which are not organized along family or blood lines so much as by a social hierarchy with a dominant male and female at the top and submissive animals at the bottom. With this structure, strange dogs can be accepted into a pack as long as the new dog submitted to the dominant animals. She still looked confused. What did all this have to do with the aggressive dog?

This dog was escaping from his confines and "attacking" her because the dog had no functional social structure; it was not an accepted member of a pack. This is a very unpleasant situation for a dog, and such dogs normally have behavioral problems. She still looked at me as if I had two heads.

I described the existence of "lone wolves" and how these animals are usually profoundly disturbed creatures since they are incapable of achieving dominance inside a pack, yet for one reason or another are unable to accept a submissive position either. Lone wolves suffer from not being a member of a functional pack, and usually have a much shorter life span. This did not work either.

I explained to her how my dog, when he was just entering doggy adulthood, had once turned on me while I was walking him on a leash. The dog actually squared off against me and began to growl at me. It required me to use exceptional, perhaps some would describe it as brutal, force to bring the dog back under control. However, once I had established my dominance over the dog, he rolled over and showed me his tummy, and I scratched it. All was forgiven. The girl was shocked by the fact that I had used brute force against my own dog, but she then said, "He knew you loved him though."

I shook my head. No. I explained that when a dog rolls on his back and shows his tummy, he is not looking for love so much as showing submission. When you scratch his tummy, if the dog is happy it is because that is a sign that the dog has been accepted as a submissive member of a functional human-dog social structure. If I had reacted to his reasonable challenge to my authority in anything other than with an unequivocal show of force and dominance, far from being comforted, the dog would have been in a crisis. If I had tried to reason with the dog, tried to sooth his temper with soft words, or consoled him in some other ineffective manner, far from be comforted, the dog would have been confused. His challenge would not result in him becoming the dominant individual in our Family/Pack, yet I would have lost my position as the dominant male. Such a situation would be profoundly troubling to a dog since the dog would have his entire social structure removed in one stroke. There is nothing unusual about a dog challenging the dominant male, nor is there anything unusual if the dominant male defends his position with force. Such challenges take place and actually serve to confirm the social structure of the pack. What is unusual for a dog is to have a leaderless pack. I lost her again.

I realized then that it was very unlikely that I was gong to be able to explain to this little girl how to structure a functional human-dog social structure in light of the fact that she apparently had no understanding of how a functional human-human social structure works (and probably no interest in the subject other than to get the unruly dog from jumping on her). Her family is probably as dysfunctional as any you would see on afternoon TV, and all around her there is only examples of failure and hopelessness, all a midst a wealth and luxury so profound as to be startling. Why should she understand these things? Why should she or anyone really care???

Human social structures are similar to a functional dog pack, but are much more complex. Although there is evidence of the same hierarchical structure of dominance, the need to constantly express dominance and submission seems to be less pronounced among humans. Perhaps the most interesting aspect of human social interaction is the way that humans can create ad hoc social structures on the fly with the relationships of dominance sometimes changing according to different circumstances. For example a football team will usually have a dominant member who is best suited to lead the team, and this is usually the quarterback. Now take these same individuals off of the football field, and put them into a study group in the library, and a different member of the group may become the dominant figure, or perhaps even an outsider will become the dominant individual based on his or her superior characteristics in that field of endeavor. The same might happen if the group decides to play basketball or go shopping. This ability to form fluid ad hoc functional social structures seems to be a rare if not unique characteristic of human behavior when compared with other social structures found in nature.

However, there is something that has developed in the last 50 years that is even more unique: the Dysfunctional Social Structure. During the last 50 years or so, particularly in Europe and North America, humans have been able to develop a social structure that goes against every aspect of natural human behavior as witnessed and documented over several millenniums, if not longer. No longer are human social structures dominated by individuals who control and manage the group according to a superiority/competitive factor that serves to benefit each member individually and the group as a whole, but now we have social groups that seem to form for no reason other than for the detriment of the individuals and the group.

These Dysfunctional Social Groups now permeate all aspects of our society. We have dysfunctional families that are incapable of raising children into self-sufficient adults, schools that are incapable of teaching students how to read and write, youth gangs that serve no purpose other than to put young men and women in harms way while venting youthful energies on drugs and other anti-social activities, governments that are incapable of performing their basic governing tasks, etc. Yet instead of such social organizations failing entirely in light of their inherent noncompetitive character, the expected result in nature, somehow they thrive in this new utopia of socialist equality and multiculturalism.

When I state that these dysfunctional social groups are noncompetitive, I am not being moralist so much as trying to be factual. If a football team, a company, or any other organization operated like this, it would lose at every encounter with a more functional group. As such, one would think that this type of structure would disappear of its own inefficiencies. But this is not the case. We see that this dysfunctional behavioral pattern seems to repeat itself across society from the family, to schools, to the work place, and into politics. Admittedly, politics have always attracted the dregs of society, but the influence of modern dysfunctional politicians seems to increase as their incompetence and corruption become more apparent.

What is one to make of this situation? Have we as a society discovered a way to breed a healthy and diverse non-conformity while at the same time finding a way of propping up society in the absence of the support structures usually associated with more traditional and functional norms? Or is it just a matter that the support beams of our society are so strong and deep that they resist the internal rot of a corrupted society (but for how long)? If it is the former, then I suppose we need to celebrate the "diversity" that many traditionalists would confuse with anti-social perversity. However, if it is the latter, then we may discover that those ancient beams underlying our social structure require more than an occasional nod and a splash of paint to keep them standing. Without constant maintenance and care our social structure may collapse when those ancient pillars can no longer support the weight of a wholly dysfunctional society.

Unfortunately, History suggests that the latter is the case. Societies that have abandoned their social norms in favor of "dysfunctional" norms have tended to collapse. The most obvious example is Rome, but I actually think Athens is a more appropriate case. During the Persian Wars, Athens was almost destroyed when the Athenians were forced by the Persians to abandon their land and city, and virtually all of their possessions, and take to their ships in defiance. Although defeated by the Persians, the Athenians had not abandoned their traditional views on courage and creativity. As the Persians captured their city, and plundered their possessions, the Athenians stood offshore watching and waiting. And when the opportunity presented itself, outnumbered and with water-logged leaky ships, the Athenians courageously struck a desperate blow and destroyed the Persian naval forces supporting the ground forces. Without a navy to support their ground troops, Persia was forced to withdraw from Athens. The Athenians had won the battle based upon a profound faith in their courage and intelligence, and soon Athens was the leader of a coalition of Greek states that defeated the Persians and forced them to reluctantly return their many conquests among the Greek speaking cities and states of Europe and Asia.

Over time Athens became not only the leader of the Greek speaking peoples in an alliance against Persia, but the leader of an Empire that influenced the entire Mediterranean. When

Athens was challenged by fellow Greek city states led by Sparta, Athens was able to single-handedly stand up to all enemies for over 40 years. Even after Athens was defeated by the Spartans, and its empire was stripped from it, Athens recovered quickly and became once again a powerful Greek city state, if not a conquering one. Athens became a center for commerce, education and the sciences.

However, it was not the Persians, or the Spartans, or any external enemy that finally brought the Athenians low, but the Athenians themselves. Somewhere along the way, the proud Athenian virtues of courage and intelligence were replaced with cynicism and sophistry. When the Romans came to take control of Athens there was not only a complete lack of opposition, but there was not even the remotest spark of a desire to be independent. The population of Athens was larger than during the wars with Persia and Sparta, yet the Athenians were unable to raise more than a thousand men for a state militia that was unable to even defend its citizenry against internal lawlessness. When the Romans entered Athens they were probably welcomed as a source of law and order, if not as outright liberators. For the Athenians had been conquered and defeated prior to the arrival of the Romans by an internal enemy that had rotted the very core of Athenian society.

In the words of Cicero:

> *"A nation can survive its fools, and even the*
> *ambitious. But it cannot survive treason from*
> *within. An enemy at the gates is less formidable,*
> *for he is known and carries his banner openly. But*
> *the traitor moves amongst those within the gate*
> *freely, his sly whispers rustling through all the*

*alleys, heard in the very halls of government
itself."*

By the time the Romans entered Athens, the enemy within had done its work so thoroughly that there was nothing left of Athens other than aged buildings and the intellectual musings of those who had abandoned the hope of ever accomplishing anything. Athens was like an old empty abandoned museum with paint flaking off the deserted walls. One looked inside wondering what the place must have been like in its prime.

If someone can point to a nation or society that has survived the treason of Dysfunctional Social Structures, then I would like know about it. I doubt our society will do any better than Athens if we cannot defeat the rot from within.

Is the USA still a Constitutional Republic

I am often criticized for being a conspiracy nut when I say that the USA is no longer a self-governing Constitutional Republic but instead an Oligarchic Fascism ruled by elites made up of, and controlling, government, business, the media, and academia.

The thing is this is not really a conspiracy in the traditional sense of the definition, and I suppose my definition of 'fascism' is not 100% in agreement with the classic definition either:

> *A system of government marked by centralization of authority under a dictator, stringent socioeconomic controls, suppression of the opposition through terror and censorship, and typically a policy of belligerent nationalism and racism. Wordnik*

Although I acknowledge that this definition works very well for Nazi Germany and the last stages of Fascist Italy, it excludes a number of important examples. Spanish fascism does not really fit. Neither do the fascist parties that dominated most of South America during the 20th Century, or the Arab Nationalist movement which was based upon early Italian fascism.

My definition of fascism is broader:

> *A system of government that uses centralized government power and comprehensive societal control instead of democratic methods to achieve its political ends which usually involve some aspects of nationalism, religion, culture, and ethnicity.*

In my definition fascism does not have to be a brutal dictatorship. This is because I believe the primary aspect of fascism is the centralized government and party control that extends into every aspect of society combined with the stated ends of nationalism, religion, culture, and ethnicity of some sort. As such democratic fascism is very much a possibility as is oligarchic fascism which is what I think we have in modern America.

So finally what is an 'oligarchy'?

> *Government by a few, especially by a small faction of persons or families. Wordnik*

So when I say that the USA is no longer a Constitutional Republic and has become a Fascist Oligarchy I am not referring to Nazi Germany, goose stepping soldiers, or concentration camps. Nor am I suggesting a vast conspiracy. Rather it is simply the natural result of the central government growing too large, and the Constitutional checks and balances becoming ineffective or obsolete.

We are not "ruled" by an iron willed cabal of co-conspirators so much as by a collection of elite special interests that are quite happy with the status quo. Big Business likes being able to use the government to erect obstacles against smaller nimbler competitors. They also like being able to collude with the political parties to extract government contracts and benefits. Bureaucrats and politicians are happy to be able to extract extortion money from Big Business, Unions, and other special interests to line their pockets. The Media and Academia do their job of acting as a holy priesthood selling the masses on the "justice" of the system. All these "elites" are potential mini-dictators in competition to control the system, not a uniform monolithic conspiracy directing every aspect of the system. They cooperate when it suits their interests, and compete with each other to obtain added power and benefits when that is more advantageous for them. Sometimes these elites are incredibly ineffective due to their competing interests.

This is really nothing new. It is the primary way societies have been run for thousands of years. What was different was the brief period when the USA was NOT run like this because of the existence of limitations on central government authority imposed by the US Constitution. Those Constitutional limitations that once deprived the ruling elites of access to the power and authority of a dominant central government are now gone. Also absent is society willing to defend its freedoms and liberties from these opportunistic elites.

This process is as natural as a river changing its course over time.

The Late Roman Republic showed these same traits. Corruption, conspiracies, coups, fraud, financial mismanagement, foreign adventurism, etc. Eventually the Republic collapsed. What is happening in America is not the result of some grand confederacy of dunces joining together to bring down the country, but a wholly natural evolution of what happens when the central government becomes too large, the people become too soft, and the infrastructure of 'democracy' becomes wholly corrupted.

In the absence of some great event or some great leader nothing will change. Wishful thinking is not a substitute for rational thought.

Stoicism in a Nutshell

Explaining the philosophy of stoicism can be difficult. Dictionary definitions focus on "indifference to pleasure or pain". Some think Stoics sit around in hair shirts whipping themselves and then rubbing salt in the wounds.

This is not stoicism.

> *Stoicism is a philosophy that tries to understand the nature human satisfaction in the world as it truly exists, and in so doing gain a sense of tranquility, appreciation, and perhaps even happiness.*

However, understanding stoicism is made difficult in part by how the ancient Stoics taught. Stoics established schools that taught a wide variety of subjects. Philosophy was just one part of what students were required to master after much difficult study. Also most of what we have from the Stoics are personal correspondence in the form of Dear Abbey type responses to a wide variety of personal questions. Reading anything from the ancient Stoics often seems like reading a collection of fortune cookie sayings.

The exception to this is a great modern book, "A Guide to the Good Life: The Ancient Art of Stoic Joy" by William B. Irvine. If you are interested in Stoicism I strongly suggest you read it.

Courage, Confidence and Competence

So here is my version of stoicism in 3 parts:

1. Live in the Now — you must learn to let go of past pain. It does nothing to help you, and may actually interfere with lessons that can be learned. You also must learn to let go of both fears and hopes for the future. You must learn to fully embrace the Now: your current situation, your current possessions, your current opportunities, and the person you are right now.

2. Understand Control — there are some things you have no power over; the weather, the past, other people, laws of nature, etc. Do not waste time and energy on things you cannot change. Instead focus on those things within your control; most notably your own thoughts, emotions, and actions. In this way you can actually improve things.

3. Understand Values through 'negative visualization' — Instead of operating with a mindset of optimism, which may often prove to be false, misleading, and disappointing, while in a calm state of mind visualize all the things that can go wrong; all the things you can lose. This will accomplish a number of beneficial things:

    ○ if something bad happens you have robbed it of much of its painful agonizing sting,

    ○ you will have a better chance of responding wisely and effectively since you have already considered the possibility, and

- ○ you have evaluated what is really valuable to you without actually having to lose anything helping you to better appreciate what you have.

By thinking about what can be lost, you may learn the true value of the various things in your life — what you can live without and still survive and perhaps even prosper, and perhaps what you cannot or should not do without.

There is a lot more to Stoicism, and a lot of fancy words to explain things, but that is my version of *Stoicism in a Nutshell*. It is always dangerous to try to put things into nutshells since usually only nuts are in nutshells.

Stoicism: Negative Visualization vs Negative Attitude

We are inundated with endless streams of advice telling us we need to visualize our dreams and desires, and to always have a positive attitude about our future.

The ancient and modern Stoics do not believe this is wise. They believe that a "positive attitude" will more likely lead to disappointment and disillusion since life is filled with ups and downs, and an overly optimistic view of life will lead to unrealistic expectations.

> *"Misfortune weighs most heavily on those who expect nothing but good fortune." Seneca*

Instead Stoics advise the practice of 'negative visualization'. Negative visualization involves the calm consideration of what would happen if you lose the things you have. Negative visualization accomplishes many things:

1. Loss loses its painful sting when it has already been considered as a possibility.

2. By considering the bad things that can happen one is better prepared to act positively when they occur.

3. Considering the loss of what you currently possess helps to create a greater sense of gratitude for those

things. It is an old saying that you never appreciate the things you have until you lose them. Through negative visualization you renew your appreciation for the things you have without having to lose anything. In other words you will have an 'attitude of gratitude' for the things you have rather than an unhealthy obsession over things you do not.

4. Finally negative visualization helps you to compare the value of things. What things can you do without and still prosper? And what things do you really need? Negative visualization helps us to differentiate the two.

Positive visualization on the other hand encourages us to fantasize about things that we do not have creating a risk of false expectations and the loss of appreciation for the things we do have. This is a recipe for unhappiness since no matter what you have, you will always want more. And the more you want, the less you will appreciate what you have.

People often respond to the concept of negative visualization with accusations that it is just a bad attitude. There is a big difference between having a realistic 'attitude of gratitude' created by negative visualization, and having a negative attitude; that is a belief that everything is bad and likely to get worse.

Negative visualization creates the very opposite of a 'bad attitude'. After considering the loss of everything you will often experience a profound sense of satisfaction with what you have. Pursuing positive visualization on the other hand can leave you helpless when things go wrong, and profoundly disappointed when your unrealistic expectations fail to materialize.

Negative visualization is not the same thing as having a negative attitude. Far from it, negative visualization creates an organic sense of calm, harmony, and gratitude which empowers the person to to appreciate what he or she has now, and overcome obstacles that may lie ahead.

A Letter

I had the worst dream last night. I dreamed that I was probably about 20 years younger. I was in my early 30s. I was with my mother. But she was not my mother. She only looked like my mother, but was someone else. A horrible shrill irritating harpy whose only purpose was irritating me and everyone around her. We were doing some shopping, and she was complaining about everything, and I was walking alongside her trying to not say anything. Just nodding and muttering things to myself and to her. Then suddenly an old man came up to me and called my name, "Alex?" He was the dirtiest hobo I had ever seen. He had a scraggly gray beard, no teeth, rheumy clouded eyes, covered in cuts and bruises, and he smelled terrible. I couldn't recognize who this man was. Then I did. It was my father. He tried to hug me, but then my mother shrieked and launched herself at him like a rabid pit bull dog. Hitting him, scratching him, biting him, and she pushed him into the street. He was hit be a bus, then my mother launched herself on him and kept beating him. I pulled her off him; she was insane. There was this burning craziness in her eyes and she was just yelling incoherent nonsense that I couldn't understand. She was covered in my father's blood. I took her to a nearby bathroom and ordered her to start cleaning herself and she obeyed, and then I rushed out to my father. He was alive. His hand was shredded and his arm was coming out of his shoulder as if his shoulder no longer existed. I pulled him out of the street and tried to do first aid on him, but he just looked up into my face and smiled this toothless idiot smile. Then I woke up.

That was not my father or mother. Those were my fears. Am I turning into that man who I identified as my father? I will leave the issue of what my mother represented to another time. Of course I am not turning into a ragged deranged hobo, but obviously that is my fear. I do not want to be like that. Not even in a small way. I don't want to take even the smallest shuffle in that direction. That IS NOT WHAT I WANT!!!

Then I thought about something: what do I want? I don't know. I am 53 years old and I really don't know what I want. I don't want a new car, or a new house, not a pretty girlfriend, or fancy clothes. I don't want very much of anything. I suppose there are a few things I might want, but not enough to actually go out and get it. I want a little farm where I can escape from the world – putter in the garden, read some, write some, etc. I could get such a place for a few thousand dollars here and maybe spend a few thousand dollars more on building a basic little hacienda. But I don't. So I guess I really don't want it after all. The best way to judge someone, including yourself – perhaps particularly yourself, is by what the person does not what the person says.

Then I realized what I wanted: the same thing I have wanted for a very long time – to share my life with my family. As I look back on my life that is what I have tried to do, but I haven't been very successful. And as I look back to the time when I was in my 30s I realize I had a lot more dreams and desires then, some of which I successfully achieved and some that I failed to achieve, and that none of them really mattered very much. The ones I have achieved now seem mostly sterile and false, and the ones I failed to achieve seem pointless and tedious. But I would still like to share some experiences with you and your sister – like we used to when you both were younger. Go camping, travel around, visit new things, etc. Again, my efforts at this have been stymied at every turn. I wonder if I am just wasting my time, or if I am doing it all wrong. Or both.

So I am not wholly without wants and desires, just rather hopeless about ever achieving them, and unwilling to replace them with meaningless crap that I don't even want.

Should I want more? Should I want more stuff – the stuff that everyone tells me I should want? More money (if for only to make sure I never become that desperate hobo in my dream)? I don't know.

This brings me to another thought: I am wearing a fake rolex I bought awhile back for giggles. I like it quite a lot. It is a very nice watch, and I do not regret spending the $150.00 on it. Of course I could buy a real one. I have the $5,000. In fact if I shopped around I could probably buy a nice rolex like this one for a few thousand or so at a pawn shop. I suppose it would be at least as nice as this one, perhaps better. But I don't. I like this watch enough to spend $150 on it, but not enough to spend $5,000.

There are other ways I would like to spend that money that might make me happier. Even if I don't exactly know what they are right now. Maybe I will get around to buying that farm, or taking a trip with my kids, etc. Or maybe just invest it into some apartments so that I can rent them out and make a little money – not what I want so much as making sure what I don't want doesn't happen.

So right now I would prefer to keep the $5,000 in my bank account until the time comes when I know what are the things that I want. Then I will have the money I need to buy those things. I can wait. Right now a $5,000 watch is just not as important as the possibility of finding what I really want and having enough money to buy it.

Does that sound crazy to you? It seems crazy to me to buy a watch that I really don't want to impress people I really don't like, and then risk not having the money to buy what I really do want… whatever the hell that might be.

Freedom vs Freedom

During our chat I think you thought we were talking about money. I thought we were talking about freedom. There are essentially only two types of freedom. If you want one thing you tend to lose another. That is because nothing is free. For example the traditional idea of freedom is liberty to do what you want when you want how you want. Freedom from external control. But this type of freedom comes with huge responsibilities and trade-offs. To be free like this requires you to show tremendous discipline, and you have to choose between different things since you cannot have everything.

You have to say NO to yourself and to others in order to be able to be free like this. Otherwise you will end up being impoverished, or enslaved to a job of some sort. Or worse, you will seek other ways of living without responsibility and you will end up in jail.

Both situations result in the exact opposite of freedom. That is why this type of freedom comes with a very high price in responsibility. You have to be careful not to spend more money than you have available to you. To accept that if you want one thing you are going to have to give up a lot of other things. You will need to limit your behavior so as to avoid unnecessary entanglements and complications. Otherwise it is just a matter of time before you lose your freedom one way or another.

There is of course another type of freedom: Freedom from Responsibility. And this is not necessarily a bad thing. But it is exactly the opposite of the first freedom. To be free from responsibility you have to surrender all your other freedoms to someone or something else. You have to give up CONTROL of your life, and obey what others tell you to do.

The most obvious example of this is the sailor in the Navy. Sailors are not usually known for their responsible fiscal behavior when they are let off the ship on shore leave. They spend their money like drunken sailors (but not like politicians – since the drunken sailor stops spending money when the money runs out).

This works out for sailors because they have no bills to worry about. The Navy takes care of everything for them. They have a place to sleep, food to eat, even clothes to wear. And if they stay in the Navy long enough the Navy will even take the responsibility of saving money for them for their retirement. But the sailor pays a very high price for this "freedom from responsibility". The sailor gives up 100% control over his body, and to a certain degree also his thoughts. He goes where the Navy tells him to go, he does what the Navy tells him to do (no matter how stupid and wasteful), he wakes up when the Navy tells him to wake up, and he eats exactly what the Navy tells him to eat.

As I said, all freedom comes with a cost. Freedom from external control requires you to be disciplined and careful with your choices regarding money, friends, and life in general. Freedom from responsibility on the other hand is the exact opposite requiring you to surrender control of your life to something else so that you do not have to ever be responsible for most of your own decisions. Both have advantages and disadvantages. I believe it is possible to be happy choosing either type of freedom, BUT YOU MUST ACCEPT THE PRICE!

If you decide you want to be free in the traditional definition, free from external control and at liberty to do what you desire, then you must be very responsible so that you do not fall into the traps of slavery that are set all around you. If you are irresponsible with your money, refuse to accept that you must make choices between different desirous things, you will soon be in poverty, and in poverty you will have little or no freedom.

If on the other hand you decide you want to be free from responsibility, then you must submit to the will of some external force in order to obtain this freedom which many desire.

If you try to have your cake and eat it too, or in other words you want to be free from external control and at liberty to do what you want, but you do not want to be responsible for you money and your own behavior, you will lose all your freedoms.

You have a lot of time to consider how you want to spend your life. If the choices you made in the past were foolish and wrong because you refused to accept that there were prices to be paid for everything, you have the chance now to make better choices. I hope is that you do exactly that: MAKE INTELLIGENT CHOICES FOR YOURSELF. Don't run away from difficult choices, accept them.

If you want to be really free, at least as I define it, you are going to have to embrace personal responsibility for your actions. This will reward you with a level of freedom that I think will result in profound happiness and satisfaction in your life.

But if you do not want to embrace personal responsibility then please make the wise and honest choice and choose an acceptable form of Freedom from Responsibility. The Navy is not the only option out there, but if you choose this course understand and accept that you are giving up your other freedoms. You are going to have to do what other people tell you to do and to keep doing it until they tell you to stop.

Think about how you want to live your life, make the choice, and then go out and do it. Be honest with yourself. Everything has a price. Nothing is free. You are the only person you really have to answer to. Make whatever choice you think will make you happy and then stick to it. If it turns out you are wrong and you don't like the choice you made, you can change your mind which of course will require you to change your behavior. What ever choice you make, be willing to pay the price. I suspect if you do so you will be happier and more satisfied regardless of which choice you make. If you refuse to accept this simple equation, that you have to pay a price for one type of freedom or another, then you are going to lose everything. I would hate to see that.

How to Get Rich!

You asked me a very good question: How can I get rich?

I did my best to answer but I fear you may have been asking the wrong person. I am not rich. What I have obtained in my life is from a combination of hard work, saving my money for years, and inheriting from my parents. So when I answered, I tried to think about what another rich person advised me to do. That was my father.

His advice was what I gave you:

1. Stop losing money. That is stop spending more money then you make on living expenses. There are only two ways to do this: Make more money and spend less money. I believe this is something you need to work on.

2. Save your money until you have enough to invest. Get yourself a nest egg. You already have this.

3. Invest your money in things you believe in (after thorough investigation and thinking) that will result in profit and thus wealth: education, stocks, real estate, entrepreneurship, etc. There are a lot of ways to make money, but be careful of fast bucks and quick deals. I have lost a lot of money on that sort of thing

*** Courage, Confidence and Competence***

My father pointed out that any of these choices may prove successful, but that he had never had much luck with real estate and entrepreneurship, and had only been successful in the stock market and that was only after he started doing numbers 1 and 2. So that is what he did. He stopped spending money he did not have (in my Dad's case that was on horses, cars, restaurants, etc.), he saved up a small amount to invest (and was constantly adding to this amount on a monthly basis from his salary), and he scrupulously studied several hours a day from various sources and invested in stocks he believed in. He made a lot of money.

In my case I must look back and evaluate my successes and failures. I have had some success in the stock market and in real estate. My investment failures have been in education and in entrepreneurship. These failures have resulted in the gains from my successes being drained off to pay for the failures.

So what should you do? Well continue asking that question. I am flattered that you asked me, but find people who have actually made money and try to learn from them.

The good news is that you can be very charming and people will talk to you if you let them. Frankly, most people are dying to tell you their success story (particularly rich people) and if you just listen you will get the information free of charge. But be careful. What worked for them may not work for you. And be very cautious about following other people's advice (particularly when it is inconsistent with what they did to succeed). My father advised me to invest in education and start a law office and that was just terrible advice, at least for me. I don't want to give you bad advice.

That aside here is my advice: find a way to stop losing money (number 1 above). Right now you are bleeding from your expenses being higher than your income. Part of that involves some temporary issues which will pass, but part of that is your own refusal to spend less and make more. Solve that. It should be easy if you swallow your pride a bit.

Next, think about what you are good at and what you could do to make money. That will require a great deal of research and experimentation. Be ready to fail. That is how you find out you are wrong, and need to find something else. Be willing to cut your losses and move on. Never chase a bad investment – never pour good money after bad.

With that in mind avoid "betting it all" on one big deal. Protect your assets. The secret to making money in poker is to win big, lose small. That, in my humble opinion, is good advice in all things related to money. However, I know some would say you need to be "passionate" and commit 100% to what you believe in like Elon Musk, etc. That may have worked for him, but from my experience there are a lot more guys who lose everything that way. And if you actually look at what these billionaires did, they generally did not blindly chase their passions, but prudently investigated, invested piece-meal a little at a time often in a variety of different investments, and only after they were convinced it would work did they put everything on the line.

I advise moderation. Never put all your eggs in one basket. Always have an escape route planned. Always keep enough cash handy to save yourself and those you love. Never be too confident in yourself or those around you. And be lucky. You can make yourself lucky by constantly being prepared. When that good luck strikes (some people call it opportunity), you need to be ready and able to respond positively. If you are drowning in debt and distracted by daily issues, you will not even recognize the opportunity that presents itself to you until it is too late if at all.

Decency

I have been trying to understand what I dislike about modern America, and perhaps understand better what I crave: decency.

Decent people are not perfect, are not always right, are not always even very smart. But they are not filled with… indecency. It is not a religious issue (although some religion does seem to help to promote decency), it is not a racial issue, it is not a gender issue, or a sexual orientation issue. It is not a political issue.

Anyone can be decent.

It is hard to define a decent person. He or she is not someone you always agree with. Rather a decent person is someone who you can ride on a bus with and not be afraid of making eye contact with. A decent person is a stranger you meet at a cafe who you chat with over a cup of coffee. A decent person is someone who lives his life as best he can, and tries to make the world just a little bit better in some small way even if he doesn't realize he is doing it.

What happened to simple decency?

It is my opinion that the majority of the American people have lost their sense of decency. They have no problem voting for indecent individuals who promise them loot. This makes them indecent. The indecent are now in charge of this country from top to bottom (or bottom to top?). You will never convince them to give up their dishonestly obtained government benefits (whether it is individual or corporate welfare) unless you can also convince them to embrace decency and self-reliance. That will result in them losing some very real short-term financial benefits. A hard sell. Any change that could have been made in regards to reforming the system should have been made decades ago before these people became the majority.

The indecent are not stupid. They are not fools. They have cleverly gamed the system and concluded they can get more from voting for one party or another even if it involves morally corrupt practices. To get them to change their mind you are going to have to get them to change their heart.

Conservatives are very good at preaching to the choir, but not so good at preaching to the lost.

When people study about the Founding Fathers even the most adoring fans focus on the genius and inspiration found in the Declaration of Independence and the balanced approach of the Constitution. That rather ignores the miserable pettiness in which the War for American Independence was waged, and the utter failure these same men had in regards to the Articles of Confederation which was one of the worst designed systems of government ever implemented. It also totally ignores the underlying social movement toward decency and morality.

The Founding Fathers were not only worried about creating a technical system of checks and balances to insure limited government and personal liberty, but they were terrified that the American people were not fit for freedom; that they were too self-indulgent and ignorant to avoid the pitfalls of representative government.

While Jefferson, Washington, Adams, Franklin, Hamilton, et al were out devising clever systems to run the government there was a grassroots movement where people were encouraged to return to abandoned churches and schools, and to raise themselves and their children to a higher moral level. The Founders believed that a Free People had to be a Decent People.

To what degree it succeeded is a matter for debate.

When I look at America I do not see a country filled with decent people. Quite the opposite. There are pockets of decency here and there, but the culture seems to have been hijacked by indecency. Even if the intricacies and technical details of a Constitutional limited government can be restored, is it possible to restore decency to an indecent country?

How to be a Lying Turd

Humans are particularly dishonest creatures. We are almost always lying. Mostly to ourselves. This is because the secret to being able to lie convincingly is to first convince yourself that the lie is true. This is not easy, but there are ways to do it:

1. Dismiss—When ever you hear or see information that does not conform to your narrow narrative you must simply dismiss it: "That information is not important or relevant to me!" When facts get in the way of your story that means the facts are not important. Move on!

2. Distort—You should never acknowledge facts that go against your narrative, but sometimes you just cannot dismiss them as unimportant and irrelevant. Instead you must distort what the facts actually mean: "The facts don't really mean what you think they mean! They mean something else!" Essentially you must take the clear meaning of the facts and twist them into something entirely different, and then demand that your spin on the facts are the only truth: "Who are you going to trust; me or your lying eyes?" Repetition helps a lot during this process. It is the art of spinning. Don't give up! Just keep repeating your side of the story. Eventually you will convince yourself, and perhaps others as well.

3. Distract—If dismissing and distortion does not work, you need to start finding other things to distract yourself and other from the truth. The world is filled with interesting and totally irrelevant stories about actors getting pregnant or adopting children, athletes being arrested, etc. Focus on distracting news stories and gossip. In other words change the subject, and pretend you never heard anything.

4. Discredit—If dismissing, distorting, and distracting yourself and others from unpleasant facts does not work you are left with one last option: find someone or something to hate, and then relentlessly attack him, her, them, it, etc. This is particularly important if they are spouting nonsense such as the truth. In a pinch anybody or anything will work, but remember when you pick on a totally innocent person there is a risk that people will sympathize with him, her, it, etc., so try to find someone who is at least unattractive. Shallow stupid people enjoy seeing unattractive people being insulted and attacked. Remember, anyone who even remotely threatens to disclose the facts, even by accident, is not only your enemy, but is also a very bad person.

   Uncover (or create) embarrassing facts about their private lives in order to discredit them, attack their family and business associates with lies and innuendo. Or just call them names; fascist, nazi, hater, etc. Do anything that will discredit them—they are your enemies!

If you cannot dismiss, distort or distract the facts, you must work to discredit any source of information contrary to your narrative: "How can you believe anything from people who are so BAD!!!!??? They are EVIL!!!!" These enemies MUST BE DISCREDITED in anyway you can so that nothing they say can ever be trusted. They must not be listened to! The louder and more shrill you are the better since it helps you to block out whatever your enemy is saying. You don't want to yourself or anyone else to even accidentally hear any of that!

There you have it. The most common way most people fool themselves into believing obvious lies. It works even better if you join in with other people and follow these 4 easy steps. The larger the group the easier it is to accept lies and falsehoods. Delusion loves crowds! The best thing about being a total liar in a crowd of other total liars is that you too can be a total liar while holding yourself out as virtuous. Awesome!

The Lesson of Lot's Wife — Its not about sex

It is my opinion that people have a tendency to over simplify biblical stories, and miss the real message. In the case of the story of Sodom and Gomorrah the story becomes all about perverted sex. Just more evidence that the Bible was written by sexually uptight repressive guys looking to force their puritanical views on others.

But that is not the entire picture. I do not think that Middle Eastern nomads living 3000 years ago would have been any more interested in intruding into people's bedrooms (or tents) than people are today. And I really doubt such people would have been all that shocked by odd acts of homosexuality now and then. Yes, the biblical story is about homosexuality and perversion, but it is also about lawless violence, homosexual gang rape, robbery, and corruption of the law. The people of Sodom and Gomorrah were not just into kinky gay sex, but they were greedy, envious, lying thieves who thought nothing of violating visitors and guests in the most violent, vile, and dishonest of ways, and then hiding behind their corrupt legal system to justify it all.

Now there is a lot of debate among religious people about exactly why God destroyed Sodom and Gomorrah. Was it because they were sexually perverted? Or was it because the entire population seems to have been taken over by violent lawless criminals who preyed upon guests and visitors in the most horrible of ways; robbing, raping, killing, etc. Does it really matter?

Sodom and Gomorrah were wholly given up to immorality and evil. The citizens of these two cities cared nothing about whether their actions were right or wrong, only about whether or not they could get away with it. Their violent sexual perversity was simply the most visible and shocking characteristic of a people who had wholly abandoned the concept of morality as a legitimate guide to individual and group behavior.

So why should anyone care, and what's the deal with Lot's wife? According to the story two angels came to Lot to save him and his family from the destruction of the two towns. Lot tried to defend Sodom and Gomorrah, but he was unable to prove that the two towns didn't deserve to be destroyed. The angels led Lot and his family away to safety. Lot's future son-in-law refused to leave and was killed when the cities were destroyed. The angels instructed Lot and his family to leave and never look back. But Lot's wife had to look back. One can only wonder what she was thinking about: Was it her comfortable home filled with all the creature comforts such as posh furniture available to people 3000 years ago, or was it her stylish neighbors, sophisticated entertainment, etc. Whatever it was that caused her to look back she was turned into a pillar of salt.

I look around at what is happening in the USA and Western Europe, and Sodom and Gomorrah comes to mind. Not quite so violent and obvious, but remember, Sodom and Gomorrah was a morality tale. One must expect extremes. The Western

World has abandoned its core ideology based upon religious morality. What is left is a world defined and controlled by subjective personal desire. According to our new moral compass the greatest evil is no longer violence and corruption spawned by immorality, but 'being judgmental'. Today being judgmental is the worst of crimes. I Somehow suspect that the people of Sodom and Gomorrah were not big fans of being judgmental either.

Conservatives have choices to make. Do we stay in Sodom and Gomorrah and turn a blind eye to the evil and corruption that is all around us while enjoying our luxuries and advanced way of life, or do we turn our back on the corruption enveloping us and choose a better way of life elsewhere?

Another European Dark Age, or the Beginning of a Fourth Renaissance?

Since the end of World War II Europe has abandoned its traditional values in a fit of cultural suicidal depression brought on by the catastrophes of the twentieth century. Europe has abandoned its culture, and surrendered to Islam. Those few patches of Europe that resist these suicidal impulses are weak and isolated. Things look bad, but perhaps there is still hope.

Europeans should have realized they were in trouble in 1996 when Bill Clinton was re-elected president after a first term punctuated by constant scandal and failure. But instead they celebrated: America was becoming more like Europe. By re-electing Bill Clinton Americans abandoned the traditional values that had made America different from the jaded and jaundiced Europeans. They took their first steps towards Post-European nihilism. Perhaps Europe celebrated out of a sense of shared values (or more exactly lack of values) and a comradeship based upon shared vices, but I think most candid observers must now look back and realize that with the corruption of America came the abandonment of Europe. A strong socially conservative America was the only thing standing between European decadence and forces bent on European destruction.

Now Europe is alone, surrounded by hostile forces, rotting from within, and surrendering its cities to intolerant fanatics that know only violence and resentment. Who knows what comfort can be found in concealing these disasters in Utopian fantasies built upon political correctness?

As stated there are still a few bastions of resistance. Some countries have managed to avoid the demographic decline caused by low native birth rates, destructive socialist economic policies, and high immigration rates from incompatible cultures. Is there any hope for them? They seem to have avoided the societal suicide taking place in France, Germany, Sweden, the UK, and other more "liberal" Western countries, but they have no real solutions of their own. The are weak, isolated, and confused. They are doing little and perhaps hoping for a hero to save them. Twenty-five years ago that hero was the USA. Now America is little better than the rest of Europe, and certainly not to be relied upon.

There seems little cause for hope. The West and all its wonders are fading away. The East offers little more than technocratic competence built on feet of clay without a sense of resolve. Latin America is sinking into a miasma of socialist economic collapse and cultural degradation. Russia is acting like a resentful spoiled child running around with a loaded gun. Africa…

Are we watching the collapse of civilization? The dawning of a new Dark Age.

Perhaps not. Perhaps we are instead seeing the dawn of a new renaissance! Perhaps things just have to get worse before they can get better?

Since the fall of the Western Roman Empire there have been three periods of "renaissance" (some suggest four). The first was called the Carolingian Renaissance which took place in the 8th and 9th centuries and revived a great deal of the order that was lost after the decline and fall of Rome. The highlights of this period are the defeat of Islamic forces in the south of France and forcing them back into southern Spain, the consolidation of European power under Charlemagne, and the general restoration of culture, education, and the arts. This all came crashing down with the arrival of the Vikings. The Vikings not only destroyed kingdoms, but they also broke the societal bonds that had kept the Europeans from tearing themselves apart. In the absence of Carolingian order the Europeans fractured, and joined their Viking brethren in equally barbaric acts of savagery.

The end of the Carolingian Renaissance ushered in two centuries of decline followed by the High Medieval Renaissance which occurred in the 12th and 13th century. This renaissance is marked by enthusiastic expansion; the beginning of the Crusades, the capture of Sicily from Islam, and the successful start of the Spanish Reconquista. Western Europe was on the mend. Great universities were founded, and architectural wonders that continue to amaze us to this day were completed. Trade expanded along with literature and the arts. Unfortunately this period of advancement and revival came to an end with the arrival of a far more brutal enemy than the Vikings: the Little Ice Age. In the 13th century temperatures began to lower and agriculture in many parts of Northern Europe failed. Famines were followed by pestilence. The Black Death, only one of many chronic outbreaks of disease, killed anywhere from 30% to 60% of the population of Europe.

After another two centuries of decline we see the rise of what most people consider the "real" Renaissance. What started in Italy in the 14th century quickly expanded throughout Europe. Some suggest that the start of the Renaissance began with the defeat of the Crusades by the Arabs, and the capture of Constantinople by the Turks resulting in mass immigration of Greek scholars, craftsmen, and tradesmen into Italy. During the Renaissance European culture flowered. The arts reached new heights along with literature and the sciences. Spain was reconquered, and the Turks expelled from most of the Mediterranean Sea. Expanding trade motivated the Age of Discovery, and European ships crossed the world and established new empires (and destroyed old empires). The Age of Reason followed, arguably a natural extension of the Renaissance, and then came the Industrial Revolution which propelled Western Europe and the United States into global dominance.

Of the three renaissances the last is obviously the most important and comes with the most lasting consequences. However, just as the prior two ended with chaotic periods marked by disaster, little Dark Ages, the Renaissance seems to have ended in its own peculiar collapse. I believe the Renaissance which began in the 14th century ended during the 20th century. Not from external forces such as Vikings or bad weather, but from internal forces of hubristic self-destruction. The violence and destruction of the World Wars of the 20th century, the collapse of the European social order, and the socialist and fascist barbarism leaving millions dead from governmental genocide against their own people extinguished confidence in Western culture, and brought about the beginning of yet another Dark Age. Only this Dark Age is unlike the others. This decline is limited and almost entirely spiritual in nature. Economically and scientifically the West is more powerful than ever, but it is morally exhausted and without purpose. This spiritual and cultural collapse can be seen in the abandonment of European religions, and in the degradation and perversion found in modern arts, literature, and education.

Although clearly not a cause for celebration, this Dark Age has not ushered in an age of chaos and destruction like the others. Cities are not being sacked, populations are not being exterminated, and scientific and educational advancements, instead of being lost or ground to a halt, accelerate onward. This means there is hope.

Perhaps this Dark Age does not have to last for centuries since their is no need to recover from any devastation. Rather there is only a need to restore and revive the spiritual strength, confidence, and enthusiasm that is now missing. In the prior Dark Ages the leaders looked to the past for motivation and encouragement. Specifically, they looked back on the glories of the Roman Empire at its height. They sought to restore the marvels of Rome to improve their own conditions, even if those marvels were largely misunderstood and often exaggerated. We do not have to look that far back. We need only look back to the Renaissance to see the grandeur and glory of an ascendant all-conquering Western culture; our culture.

Courage, Confidence and Competence

We must set aside this dark nihilistic suicidal self-loathing, and return to the faith in our religions, in our ideals, in our concepts of justice and liberty, and in our well founded enthusiasm for the future! This need not be the end, but instead the beginning of an even more glorious fourth renaissance. A renaissance that can be built on faith in a religion that ended slavery, and in a culture that created revolutionary scientific advancements to the entire world.

The West must restore its belief in its purpose. What other culture can take us to the stars? Restore the environment? Create cures for incurable diseases? Clean the oceans? Feed the planet? Educate the world? Only the West.

We need only lift our head in genuine well deserved pride and see that we have more work to do.

On Having a Credo

Our friends at Merriam-Webster define a "credo" as "an idea or set of beliefs that guides the actions of a person or group."

I have been thinking on this and decided I need my own credo. My father used to have a credo: grind the bastards down. Yes, he was a bit grim sometimes, but this credo only applied to his dealings with people outside the family. Well mostly.

Now I like my father's credo. It has in it a certainty of success that I find refreshing. It also implies a purpose; every morning you must wake up with a commitment to "grind the bastards down" regardless circumstances. You must persevere. And that is what my father always did.

But that is not me.

I have been thinking about this and I realized that your credo needs to be more than just some non-sense that you mumble to yourself in the morning. It needs to be a phrase that serves to represent everything you are, everything you value, and everything you want to accomplish. So what should I choose as my credo?

I am a big believer in honoring those who are smarter and wiser than me by stealing their ideas, so here are a few famous credos that I rather like:

Courage, Confidence and Competence

*"Veni, vidi, vici" (I came, I saw, I conquered) —
Julius Caesar*

*"¡Prefiero morir de pie que vivir siempre
arrodillado!" (It is better to die on your feet than
to live always on your knees!) — Emiliano Zapata*

*"Do what you can with what you have where you
are." — Theodore Roosevelt*

*"To have much learning, to be skillful in
handicraft, well-trained in discipline, and to be of
good speech — this is the greatest blessing." —
Buddha*

*"The greatest joy for a man is to defeat his
enemies, to drive them before him, to take from
them all they possess, to see those they love in
tears, to ride their horses, and to hold their wives
and daughters in his arms." — Genghis Khan*

*"Conquering the world on horseback is easy; it is
dismounting and governing that is hard." —
Genghis Khan*

*"Victory belongs to the most persevering." —
Napoleon Bonaparte*

*"Victory is sweetest when you've known defeat."
— Malcolm S. Forbes*

"He deserves praise who does not what he may, but what he ought." — Seneca

"You should ... live in such a way that there is nothing which you could not as easily tell your enemy as keep to yourself." — Seneca

"Warriors should suffer their pain silently." — Erin Hunter

I suppose you get the idea. Everyone has an ear to hear that which resonates within.

So after much thought I have decided this would be my credo:

Never reward kindness with cruelty, and never reward cruelty with kindness.

At least for today.

Why be a Prepper?

What makes someone a Prepper?

A few comments from the Internet:

> *"A prepper is someone who is uncomfortable relying on others for the basics of survival and protection."*

> *"A Prepper is a person who takes Personal Responsibility and Self Reliance seriously."*

> *"A Prepper is an individual or group that prepares or makes preparations in advance of, or prior to, any change in normal circumstances or lifestyle without significant reliance on other persons (i.e., being self-reliant), or without substantial assistance from outside resources (govt., etc.) in order to minimize the effects of that change on their current lifestyle."*

> *"...most of us are prepping in order to become more self-sufficient ... for whatever reason."*

> *"...different folks are going to focus on different things. The common thread though is that all preppers are concerned citizens and they are all preparing for something..."*

A Prepper, it would seem, is a person who is preparing for some event in the future, or perhaps even some event that is taking place right now. I know some would find the word "fear" distasteful, but that is the heart of the matter. We all have fears. Some of them are reasonable, and some of them are not.

Is it "reasonable" to prepare yourself for obviously foreseeable "reasonable" risks? Well only a fool would say no to that, but sadly many do.

What about preparing for risks that may be less likely, less "reasonable"? Preppers would respond that being prepared is a good thing, even if the likelihood of something happening is slim. The process of preparing for one risk will most likely make you more prepared to respond effectively to other risk.

But at what point does preparing for an "unreasonable" risk distract you from preparing for other more "likely" risks?

Several years ago I started a website to try to sort these things out. My initial concern was less about preparing for natural and man-made disasters, and more about the slow yet consistent political crisis taking place in the USA and other "Free World Countries". Although I appreciate the importance of being prepared in the event of some natural disaster, I am more concerned about being prepared for a political disaster. A disaster that is not in the future, but one that has been slowly taking place over the last fifty years, and which may very well get worse in the future. Much worse.

My fears are that political and social changes will take place that will require more than a bug-out bag with 72 hours of supplies, more than a pre-arranged safe haven within a few hours of our homes, and more than a hidden bunker in the countryside where we can escape and ride-out the crisis.

I fear that the USA and other Western countries may possibly become unsafe for those who love and demand liberty for themselves and their families.

Is this a "reasonable" fear? What is the likelihood of the USA becoming a tyrannical nation that oppresses its own people? Denying its own people justice? Robbing its own people of their property? Depriving its own people of their Rights?

Some would say that these are ridiculous fears. Others would say they have already become reality, and we have simply not opened our eyes to recognize the fact. Yet others would take the middle ground: it is a possibility, but not yet a reality.

If you are one of the people who believes that these fears are legitimate to one degree or another, what are you doing to prepare? What good is a bug-out bag if there is nowhere to go? What good is a safe-haven if your enemy has the resources to hunt you down and root you out? What if there is no place to go that is safe and secure inside your own country?

The simple answer is that you are going to need to be prepared to leave the country. Where are you going to go? Are your financial resources going to be safe?

Are you prepared?

Radical Islam is not caused by Socio-Economic Injustice

The old guard of hard core Marxists that are now in control of the Leftist political movements in the West as well as the Western bastions of "higher education" retain their romantic conviction that everything that is bad in the world is caused by "economic and social injustice" and therefore can be addressed by Marxist ideas of restoring "economic and social justice". They believe this in the same way that all fanatics cling to their faith even in the face of the most obvious facts to the contrary.

In the case of the threat of Radical Islam, these old guard Marxists cling to their belief that if we can just provide better economic opportunities and perhaps better education and hygiene to the bedraggled Islamic societies and nations across the globe the threat can and will be averted. This completely ignores the basic facts involving Radical Islam, an attitude the Left tends to take in all matters. They are convinced that the best policy is to ignore facts that are contrary to Leftist political convictions and eventually they will just go away.

The rise of Radical Islam has nothing to do with "socio-economic injustice" but about long standing issues regarding Islam and its place in the world — The Chronic Historical Decline of Islam. There are two axes of conflict involving this threat to Islam:

1. The response within Islam to the threat, and

2. The response from outside of Islam to Islam itself.

The Conflict Within Islam

I think it is useful to point out that Radical Islam is a relatively new phenomena that has only gained preeminence within Islam over the past 50 years. This can be seen as encouraging since it shows that Islam was not always like this, and thus one can hope for Islam to return to its less radical form. Sadly there is no evidence to suggest that such hope will be rewarded.

Radical Islam takes many different forms among different groups within Islam, but its origin lies in one and only one historical fact: for the past 500 years Islam has been in decline. This is an objective fact that is not based upon "socio-economic injustice". The Islamic world has been asking itself one question:

What went wrong?

There have been two opposing responses within Islam to this question. The first suggests that Islam became too rigid and closed-minded and thus failed to advance technologically and socially compared to the West. The second suggests that Islam abandoned its "old" fundamental ideas (ideas that never actually existed in the "good old days" of Islamic ascension, but who wants to quibble with spitting rabid fanatics who will cut off your head with a dull knife?)

Among the first group we saw the rise of modernist reformers like Mustafa Kemal Ataturk who wanted to see Turkey and other Islamic societies embrace the modern world in a more secular manner and in that way restore the Islamic World to ascendancy. Among the second group we saw the rise of the modern sects of Radical Islam which preach that only through a "return" to ancient Islamic ideals and practices would Islam be saved.

To put it simply, the Modernists failed to deliver on their promises. They failed to reverse the historical decline of Islam. What we see today is the victory of the Radicals over the Modernists and it is very difficult to see how any "moderates" are going to overcome the Radicals. The Radicals have had some very real successes in expanding and strengthening Islam whereas the "moderates" can only offer rather timid responses to a longstanding decline. Perhaps if "moderate" Muslims, instead of running off to San Francisco, Paris, and Berlin to write articles about the horrors of modern societies, would unpack their grandfathers old Kalashnikovs and go out and fight for their beliefs things would be different? Or perhaps they would just be dead? I don't know.

The Conflict Outside of Islam

The next axis of conflict involves the response to the threat of Radical Islam from outside of Islam. From historical perspective we can see that vibrant, strong, and confident societies seem to have fewer problems resisting and repulsing Islamic advances, whereas moribund, weak, and uncertain societies have great difficulties.

During the initial rise of Islam, Islam attacked and defeated two weak and decadent empires: the Sassanid Persians and the Byzantine Romans. The Sassanids were completely destroyed and replaced by an Islamic Caliphate, and the Byzantines were devastated by the loss of key provinces that left it weak and vulnerable. The Islamic armies then spread across the ruined remains of ex-Roman North Africa with little opposition, and invaded the divided and disintegrating ex-Roman provinces of what is now Modern Spain. They were stopped in the South of France by a tenacious fighter named Charles Martel (Charles the Hammer) saving Europe from Islamic domination.

I think it is fair to state that Islam rose up at a most propitious time. The 7th century delivered to Islam a Roman Empire that was shrunk and splintered, a Persian Empire corrupt and leaderless, and a Western Europe that was at the ebb of the Medieval decline, often referred to as the Dark Ages. But after the victories of Charles Martel, Europe experienced the first of three Renaissances; the rise of the Carolingians and Charlemagne during the 8th century. With Charlemagne Europe saw a resurgence of culture, learning, building, and fighting. The Muslims were decisively repulsed from the South of France and hemmed in within the southern part of the Spanish Peninsula. Christian Western Europe was on the rise and Islam was rebuffed, at least in the West. In other regions Islam continued to advance.

The young and wobbly Carolingian Renaissance came to an abrupt end with the eruption of the Vikings from the far north during the late 8th century and throughout the 9th century. Previously safe and prosperous cities were sacked and plundered, entire kingdoms destroyed. Learning and culture were set back as libraries were replaced by walls and battlements. What the Vikings did not ravage, the Europeans themselves destroyed through petty yet violent conflicts that arose out of the chaos of a collapsed social system.

Then we saw another resurgence of Europe in the 10th and 11th centuries: The High Middle Ages or the Second Renaissance. During this period was saw the partial consolidation of chaotic mini-states into the rough forms of what we today consider the nations of Western Europe. Colleges were founded, new building techniques developed, the arts encouraged, and the reason of Aristotle was combined with Christian faith to create a vibrant culture of investigation and curiosity. It was during this time that we saw further reversals to Islamic advances in Europe and the Middle East. Islam was further pushed back in Spain, was defeated in Southern Italy, and Sicily was reconquered and returned to Christendom.

This Second Renaissance came to an end as well, but not due to the depredations of Vikings (although some of them would return), but due to the attack of Mother Nature. The Little Ice Age, which began in the 13th century, brought ruin upon Northern Europe by turning what had been fertile regions into uninhabitable glaciers and tundra. Europe retracted. Greenland became the barren wasteland we see today. Famines caused massive loss of population and dislocations, and finally the Black Death and other plagues brought decimation to already suffering populations. Combine that with Mongol Hordes and we have the recipe for a massive collapse. It was during this time that the Turks began their remorseless advance against the remnants of the Byzantine Empire (which lead to the eventual capture of Constantinople which was then renamed Istanbul). Further attacks resulted in the loss of most of the Balkans. The Mediterranean became a Turkish Sea. All the gains of the Second Renaissance seemed to be slipping away.

Slowly Europe recovered even though the weather remained inhospitable compared to prior centuries. In the 14th Century the Third Renaissance began in Italy and spread through the rest of Europe. The study of the arts and sciences flourished, Spain was finally reconquered, the Turkish control of the Mediterranean wrested away, the Turkish attacks on Central Europe through the Balkans halted and eventually reversed, and the Age of Discovery began with Europeans in small wooden ships exploring the globe and bringing back riches as well as knowledge. This Third Renaissance saw Europe propelled into the Age of Reason (which just so happens to correspond with the end of the Little Ice Age — connection?), which then in turn led to the Industrial Revolution.

This is the period that the Islamic world looks on as the "beginning of the end". The period of constant decline and loss in most of the Islamic world. Perhaps this had less to do with a real decline in the Islamic world, and more to do with a relative decline compared to the rising star of Western Europe, but all the same it is the beginning of the time period that Islamic scholars consider the beginning of their great decline.

From reviewing the history of the rise of Islam in relation to the relative strength of the societies opposing Islam we can see that Islam was most successful when its enemies were suffering some sort of internal disruption and decline, and least successful when those enemies were strong, vibrant, and confident.

Where does that leave us now in the 21st century? Things are not looking good for Europe in particular and the West in general. The vibrant culture that grew out of the Third Renaissance, the Age of Discovery, the Age of Reason, and the Industrial Revolution has lost its spirit and confidence during the 20th century. The World Wars of the early 20th century left Europe physically and morally drained. The Cold War which brought the end of Communism seems to have also brought the end of the West's confidence in its own moral and ethical superiority. At the very zenith of Western power and strength we see a culture that is lost, self-loathing, and without purpose or direction, abandoning traditional beliefs and mores and embracing all manner of self-destructive behavior.

The destructive conflicts of the 20th century have sucked the life out of Europe and Western Culture even as it brought Europe and America to the heights of scientific progress, cultural advancement, and political and military power.

It is in this moral vacuum, without confidence and leadership from the West, that we see the rise of yet another Islamic attack against the West. This attack is not one of armies and navies, but of cultures. This is because the Islamic world has no chance of contesting the West in any other way. Islam has long ceded its dominance in the arts and sciences to the West and has no interest in trying to restore its prior role as an intellectual center of learning. The militaries of the various Islamic nations have no chance to contest Western or Eastern armed forces. All they have is people. Uneducated unhappy desperate people who Islamic leaders are using to invade modern Europe and America in much the same way that the German "barbarians" invaded a decadent and collapsing ancient Roman Empire (most of these "barbarians" were either invited into the Roman Empire to help it defend itself against other threats, or they simply immigrated in small groups as the borders became porous and undefended — but that is another story).

The successes that Radical Islam is achieving against the West are not due to the strength of Islam so much as the moral weakness of the West. Europe and America have culturally collapsed into a "moral Dark Age" even as their populations enjoy unknown prosperity and technological advances.

Conclusion

As you can see from the amount of words I spent on the two elements of the conflict involving the decline of Islam and the response of Radical Islam, I believe that the real problem is not the external threat from Islam, but the internal collapse, the societal suicide, of Western culture and civilization. Islam is not defeating the West so much as picking up the pieces of what the West has abandoned. A demoralized Europe is unwilling to procreate and create the next generation of Europeans let alone defend itself and its culture from a new wave of barbarians; barbarians that have been knowingly invited in by morally bankrupt governments looking for a quick fix to reverse a looming demographic disaster. And America is proving to be a great disappointment to those who imagined it was gong to pick up the mantle of Western Civilization and lead the way to a new age of Western advancement and prosperity. It now seems very unlikely that America will lead any sort of restoration of Western Civilization, but may at best sit on the sidelines and watch as the West collapses from its own weight and lethargy.

What is to be done?

Focus less on defeating Radical Islam which is really no threat to a strong and confident culture, and instead focus on restoring the traditional values and mores that made Western Europe and America the preeminent cultural and economic powers of the world. Europe and America need a cultural restoration to reinvigorate pride and confidence. Perhaps a Fourth Renaissance. And obviously the new barbarians need to be rejected, repulsed, and removed.

A culture that does not have the moral fiber to defend itself from such open and obvious threats is perhaps a culture that does not deserve to survive.

Islam is NOT a Backwards Religion

I sometimes hear people who I profoundly respect refer to Islam as an archaic, barbaric, backward religion from the 7th century. I must respectfully disagree.

No doubt there are hideous barbaric Muslims who do the most hateful things in the name of Islam. One only need look at what happens every day in places like Afghanistan, Pakistan and other Muslim dominated nations to see the shameful degradation that people suffer under in the name of Islam. But there are hateful people in all religions.

I do not believe Islam is backward, barbaric or archaic. Don't get me wrong, I do not approve of Islam. I simply believe that Islam was and still is ahead of its time in many ways. This is because Islam is not a religion so much as an all encompassing totalitarian political movement that includes certain religious aspects and functions. In many ways Islam goes far beyond what we consider religion, and in other ways remains far less.

Almost all major religions set as a central tenet, either expressly or innately, the concept that in order to obtain ultimate truth the adherent must undertake a spiritual journey. In the end, the truth is more often than not the journey itself, not the destination.

Islam does not involve such a spiritual journey for truth. Islam literally means Submission, and Islam requires all adherents to submit wholly and completely to the will of God. That is it. No difficult soul searching. Truth is not to be found from ponderous questioning regarding the meaning of life, the universe, and everything. In Islam, truth, if such an issue is of any concern whatsoever, is to be found by simple and complete submission to the will of God, and the will of God is expressed in very practical terms within the Koran and the teachings of Islam. Ultimately, truth is a rather irrelevant proposition since it may involve understanding issues that humans are incapable of comprehending, but submission to God is a solution that requires no questioning or doubt.

In many ways, Islam is an incredibly elegant and simple system of religious practice. Once you make the great leap of faith, Islam is a relatively easy religion to follow. Islam asks for no complex rituals, no bizarre behavior (although there is plenty to be found for sure), and no unreasonable demands regarding personal purity and/or perfection. Islam does not call on the Muslim to "do unto others as you would have him do unto you" or "to turn the other cheek". Islam does not require that you learn complex rituals or recitations. Islam does not require or expect you to be particularly pure of heart or of mind. All Islam requires is that you submit to God, and that you do your very best to follow the Five Pillars of Islam:

1. That you declare yourself a Muslim by declaring that there is no God but God, and that Mohamed is his Prophet.

2. That you pray five times a day at appointed times and in the directed manner.

3. That you give charity to those in need.

4. That you observe the daily fast required by Ramadan.

5. That once in your lifetime you take a pilgrimage to Mecca.

None of these are particularly difficult to perform, but even if they are for one reason or another, as long as you tried everything is fine.

Perhaps because Islam is so clear and easy to practice, there seem to be fewer doctrinal debates as there are in other religions. No complex arguments such as those over Christian beliefs regarding the Doctrine of the Trinity, the Doctrine of Predestination, or whether the Pope truly holds the key to heaven. No endless arguments like you find in Judaism regarding the meaning of a particular word or phrase. Even when Muslims disagree, their arguments are relatively practical such as in the case of the schism between Sunni and Shia: Who should be the rightful successor to Mohamed? Shiites believed succession should pass by blood to the heir of Mohamed, and Sunnis believed succession should pass in a more democratic manner by community acceptance and approval in the manner common among the Arab tribesmen.

However, for all Islams simplicity of practice, there is one aspect of Islam that can create endless concern and consternation for the Muslim: What is required by God to go to heaven? This is not clear. Most religions provide some answer to this question, even if the answer involves extraordinary actions by the adherent. In Islam there is never certainty. A Muslim never knows if he has done enough. There is no smug suggestion that if you do one thing or accept some doctrine, that you are going to heaven. The issue is up to God, and man has no say about the ultimate judgment.

However, I believe that Islam is a totalitarian political movement buried under a thick veneer of religion. I suppose to one degree or another, one could make that accusation against virtually all religions. Clearly medieval Europe was dominated by the Catholic Church, and ancient Israel was often ruled by a Priesthood of Judges. Yet there was always a distinction between the religious power of the church to intercede between the individual and God, and the secular power of the government to manage affairs here on earth. This was the case even when those powers were held by the same entity. In Islam there is no such distinction. An Islamic nation is ruled by Sharia Law, and the government of an Islamic nation must submit itself to Islam and Sharia Law just as the individual must; without question or debate. The line between the secular state and religion simply does not exist. The closest thing that comes to mind is the modern examples of the Soviet Union under Stalin, Communist China under Mao, or Nazi Germany under Hitler where there was a similar erosion of the line between the individual and the state.

Furthermore, if Islam is more than a religion to the extent that it is more accurately a political movement giving totalitarian powers to the Islamic elite, it is also less than a religion. It is difficult if not impossible to define religion, but when one looks at some common references to religion in general, Islam seems in many ways lacking.

Islam does not attempt to explain the nature of the universe and/or the relationship between man and the infinite or divine. In fact, Islam more often then not tells the adherent to ignore such questions as they are likely to lead the Believer astray and away from submission to God. Historically Islamic philosophers who have spent too much time questioning such matters have ended their philosophical careers with their heads decorating some city wall in the Middle East. Islam is not about asking universal questions, or discovering universal truths. Islam is about total obedience to the will of God, no matter how incomprehensible that may be.

Sometimes people suggest that religion serves the purpose of helping people to become better and finer individuals by providing rules and examples that can help the believer make better decisions and improve upon his or her inherent goodness. This does not seem to be the case in regards to Islam. Following the rules and regulations of Islam is not necessarily intended to make you a better person, and there is little emphasis upon this; it is simply what you must do because the Koran and God demands it.

Another proposed purpose of religion is to connect the individual to the supernatural by providing a path upon which the adherent must travel in order to achieve that supernatural contact. But Islam discourages this line of thinking as akin to witchcraft. The Believer must simply submit and obey the will of God. If God wants you in heaven, you will go. And if not, it is the will of God.

Frankly, Islamic teaching strikes me as something closer to Marine Corps indoctrination than anything else. The Marines need to first strip the recruit of his or her sense of self so that the recruit can then be rebuilt into a functioning member of the team; a Marine. But even the Marines do not require the level of total personal abnegation that Islam requires of a Believer. Marine Corps training is intended to provide the Marine with the discipline and skills needed to perform specific tasks within the military structure, not to control each and every aspect of his or her life. When basic training is over, the Marine has his or her freedom and personal control restored. That does not happen in Islam; not only the individual but entire nations are required to permanently submit to the will of God with no possibility of release.

I believe Islam often gets a pass because it is a "religion" and we are raised to observe religious tolerance, but I think this is a mistake in the case of Islam. Islam is not a religion, but a totalitarian political movement that has destroyed the freedoms of every nation where it has taken root. Furthermore, there is no evidence that there is any possibility of reform. As such, until such time as Islam reforms itself, we must view it not as a religion that must be tolerated and perhaps even respected, but as a dangerous political movement that is determined to rob us of our personal liberties, and to destroy our way of life.

Thoughts after 2 years an expat in Tbilisi, Georgia — Mostly sadness

In 2015 I moved to Tbilisi. I am not 100% sure what I was looking for, but I think it was a home — a place where I belonged. I was also seeking to leave my life in the USA behind me. On the first goal I have been unsuccessful. Although I like Tbilisi and the Republic of Georgia, I no longer feel at home here. I think it was naive on my part to think that I could come waltzing in and just be accepted. On the second goal I have been successful. No matter how irritated I get about things here in Georgia it only takes me a few days into a visit to the USA before I want to leave. Will I stay in Georgia? I do not know. I am no longer as happy here as I was 6 months ago. Either things here have changed or I have changed; probably both. But I know I will not return to the USA. America has become a foreign country to me; more foreign than those nations I have visited over the last 2 years; Georgia, Hungary, or Bulgaria. Maybe I will never find a home. If so I must learn to appreciate the things I have. Which brings me to the issue of Georgia and me.

I read this quote in a book about the Caucasus, and it struck me as very near to the truth:

> *"If I were a symbolist, I should portray Georgia as*
> *a racehorse — palpitating, furious, rushing*
> *forward blindly, it knows not where; rearing at the*

*least check, not having yet learnt what is required
of it, or what it can do; falling at the first
slackening of the reins into fantastic, prancing
gait; a creature made for parade, and for the
pleasure of the eyes rather than utility... The most
deadly weakness of [Georgians'] nature is their
faculty of intoxicating themselves with words, their
infantile persuasion that in delivering speeches
and making gestures they are actively
accomplishing something and producing results."
Odette Keun, 1924*

I must admit that when I read this quote it struck a chord of resonance in my heart and in my mind. Georgians can be so charming and appealing with their extravagant behavior, but they can also be pig headed and irrational. Over the past 6 months Georgia has transformed from a country that welcomed foreigners to a ridiculous and often annoying extent into a country that despises foreigners and treats them like garbage. I have never experienced such a broad based social change in sentiment about anything whatsoever. My thoughts about this country and its people are now confused, and part of me feels betrayed on a very deep emotional level. I had thought I had found that elusive thing called 'home'.

Regarding the above quote I do not necessarily agree with it entirely. To the extent I find some merit in it I must acknowledge that such generalizations are always going to be false as a matter of logic. All that is required is one exception to the rule. To paint a picture of an entire ethnic group with such a broad brush is going to be false even if there are interesting aspects of truth.

We each come to any thought and opinion with our own bias. I wonder what was Odette Keun's bias, and what caused it? In my case I can attest that I have broken many of my own rules regarding judgment since arriving in Georgia and those mistakes in judgment have ended up costing me a lot of time, trouble, money, and heart ache. The mistakes are my own and not the cause of the Georgian government, the people, or the "nation" whatever that is.

First of all I broke my first rule: never fall in love with something or someone who cannot or will not love you back. Seems so obvious but is actually very difficult — when first in love if we don't outright reject unpleasant facts we twist them and turn them to appear as we desire. I fell in love with Georgia and in so doing I only saw what I wanted to see. I only saw the beauty and the wonder, not some of the less appealing aspects. As a result I have been blindsided by my own foolishness. Its like crossing the street without looking both ways. If you get hit by a car it is at least partially your fault.

Secondly, I broke my business rule as an attorney to never care more about the client's problems than the client himself. It is an easy rule to forget as you bury yourself in the facts of the case — you become not only a self-declared expert but also a guardian angel defending the rights of the client. But what if the client doesn't really care? Or doesn't really want your help? It happens a lot in the law — people who are foolish, lazy, arrogant, inconsistent, etc. tend to need lawyers more than the wise and prudent, and yet they also tend to appreciate them less. In my case I stupidly took on the problems of Georgia as my own, only to be very disappointed when Georgians seem to be lackadaisical and careless about their own concerns, and disinterested in my thoughts. BUT NO ONE ASKED FOR MY HELP. The fault is entirely my own.

So if we find some truth in Ms. Keun's statements, I think it is fair to point out that her opinions were most likely formed from some previous errors in judgment made by her, and reflect the subsequent regrets that set in. Our subjective opinions are formed from our own personal experiences that are often caused in part by ignorance, arrogance, foolishness, and stupidity.

I am no longer in love with Georgia that is clear, but neither do I hate it. I am disappointed on a very childish emotional level at what I perceive as a betrayal. But the truth of the matter is I failed myself. And now I risk allowing the same passion turned against itself to blind me further. When you are in love it is difficult to see the flaws in the object of your desires, but when that love is not returned or is rejected it is very difficult to even see the good. Am I experiencing culture shock? I don't think so. I let passion rather than reason dominate my thinking, but after more than 2 years any culture shock I experienced is gone. There are a lot of wonderful things about Georgia, and I should appreciate them. But there are also a lot of unpleasant things here and I am not sure the good outweighs the bad.

I don't know if I will stay here, or whether I will go elsewhere in search of that thing that might fill the puzzling hole within me. I recall what my father used to say, "If you are not happy where you are the fault is not in the place but in you." We will see.

The Dangerous Emergence of "Protester Culture"

Over the past decades, across the globe, there has emerged the idea that "protesting" is a valid, legitimate, and altogether natural activity when faced with unappealing election outcomes or disagreeable government behavior. This idea that "protesting" is "democratic" needs to be reconsidered, particularly the notion that protesting is somehow automatically virtuous and democratic when it may very well be the opposite.

Fair and honest elections are what define modern 'democratic' self-governing nations, not small bands of hyper-emotional ill informed and too often paid agitators protesting something or other they may not really understand or even care very much about.

Few would suggest that paid protesters opposing an otherwise valid election outcome are a healthy part of a 'democratic' system. But beyond the issue of the potential for fraud and malicious manipulation created by the use of paid protesters is the more troubling development of a "protester culture".

Again, 'democracies' in the modern sense of the term are defined by fair and honest elections that the people ACCEPT. You don't have to like the outcome every time, but you do have to accept the outcome because to do otherwise is to reject the system of self-government. This Acceptance also means that you believe the best way of altering a bad election outcome is to do a better job convincing the voters during the next election. These are the foundational principles of 'democratic' self-government. These beliefs need to be supported as matters of Faith in order for self-government to succeed. Protesting a valid and legal election because the other side won is rejecting the 'democratic' system, and embracing some very non-democratic alternatives such as rule by mobs, coups by elites, oligarchic conspiracies to manipulate or maintain the status quo, or some unpleasant combination of the above. When this happens your democracy/republic is finished.

I would point out 19th Century Mexico as a perfect example of country where democracy died from such behavior. After its independence the First Republic of Mexico, or the United Mexican States as it was then named, adopted a very well crafted Constitution that was almost immediately scrapped in favor of the above cycle of mobs, coups by elites, and oligarchic manipulation. Through out the 19th Century Mexicans carried on well mannered and well structured elections that meant almost nothing. They referred to the process as Ballots and Bullets. First there would be the election, then there would be the civil war between the party that won the election and the various parties that had lost the election. In the end only the bullets really mattered.

It is one thing for people to rise up and depose a despotic government that has shown little or no interest in the well being or the wishes of its people. It is quite another thing to rely upon "protesting" as a back up plan when you lose an election. This is what is happening in the USA, and it seems to be spreading everywhere across the globe. Right now the Armenian government is under siege by an army of 'peaceful protesters' with demands that seem to involve overturning the results of the recent election.

Why is this happening so often? Because it is a low cost, low risk, and effective tool. Even if the endless protests fail to remove the offending government from power, as in the case of the anti-Trump "Resistance", it succeeds in robbing the opposing (and winning) party of the authority and legitimacy it needs to govern. This is because along with the protesters come the biased, perhaps even corrupt, media that almost always, and perhaps even accurately, portrays these hapless protesters in a positive light.

I do not doubt that most of the protesters are well-intentioned. But regardless of their intentions, a large group of protesters is ultimately just a mob. And a mob can be manipulated easily. In reality these protesters are often nothing more than dupes of some very undemocratic forces looking to reverse the legitimate results of an otherwise valid election in which they disliked the outcome.

The danger of creating a "protester culture" is that even when the cause is just, the outcomes can no longer be trusted. Using protesters as your first option to losing an election is only one step away from using bullets. In fact the bullets are the only obvious conclusion. If the winner of a legitimate election cannot govern because of a constant state of discord caused by 'peaceful protesters', then the only option is to 'clear the streets' of the protesters using whatever force necessary. This in turn creates a motivation for the protesters to quickly ramp up their 'peaceful protests' into violent coups to overthrow the legitimate government since they know that this is where their protests are leading. Where once we had hopes of ballots determining our destinies, the bullets will end up winning one way or another. The ballots will become nothing more than meaningless adornment.

Self-government requires all parties to respect the outcome of an election.

The Difference Between Error and Evil

When does error become evil? Clearly the two tend to go together very comfortably, but they are not the same thing. You can be wrong about something without being evil, and I suppose you can also be evil while being correct. When does your erroneous prejudice concerning someone or something become evil?

Please note that I do not believe all prejudice and discrimination are erroneous or wrong. The belief that all prejudice is wrong is one of the great fallacies of modern liberal philosophy. Is it wrong to have a prejudice that fire is dangerous, even while acknowledging that it is useful? Calling such a prejudice wrong let alone evil would be the height of folly, and refusing to discriminate against fire would be nothing other than stupid. Not all prejudice is wrong.

This is the case even when we are dealing with people. If a black man saw approaching him what appeared to be an angry group of white men dressed in white sheets and carrying a rope would it be necessary for the black man to 'give them the benefit of the doubt'? Would the black man be required to create some bizarre improbable fiction to explain their behavior; perhaps they are merely trying to dry their laundry until such time as they are able to find an appropriate place to put up their clothes line? No, of course not. It would be wholly appropriate for the black man to see the approaching group of white men as a very real and personal threat to his well-being and to take appropriate action to protect himself, his family, and his property; even if those actions were discriminatory against those white men. This is because his prejudice concerning white men wearing white sheets and carrying ropes is a valid prejudice based upon real facts. Now would the black man be justified in discriminating against all white people? No, that would be an erroneous prejudice since not all white people support or approve of this behavior. Would he be justified in immediately using violent and deadly force against these men? Probably not. After all they may not have violent intentions even though their appearance is menacing; they may just be playing a prank in poor taste, or expressing a political opinion that may be hateful but not immediately dangerous. Having a menacing appearance, a bad sense of humor, or an ugly political view should not be a death sentence. But showing appropriate caution in the face of a reasonable threat would not be wrong.

If it is appropriate for a black man to have a valid and reasonable prejudice against certain white people and to discriminate against them because of this, would it be appropriate for others to have similar such valid and reasonable prejudices as well? I would say yes.

I point this out in order to distinguish between valid and reasonable prejudices and erroneous prejudices.

Thus, back to my question: When does an erroneous prejudice become evil?

My question is based upon a recent experience I had on Facebook. A 'friend' will occasionally express anti-Israel and anti-Zionist beliefs that border on and occasionally cross into Jew-Hatred. In fact I think it would be fair to say that if he is not a Jew-Hater he is certainly a Jew-Skeptic believing all sorts of conspiratorial stories concerning Jews and their control of just about everything. Another 'friend' confronted me and accused me of tacitly supporting this anti-Jew prejudice expressed by the other person because I 'associate' with him, and do not always aggressively attack this person's ideas when he states them.

(I do not use the term anti-Semitism as that term was actually coined by a radical German racialist in the 19th Century as a basis to hate Jews, and it is as inaccurate now as it was inaccurate then. It encourages false beliefs even among people who do not share those anti-Jewish sentiments. Firstly, not all Semites are Jews, and not all Jews are Semites. Judaism is a religion that is shared by many different races, cultures, and creeds.)

My immediate response was to point out that not all people who have erroneous prejudices against Jews are evil. As such, I would prefer to confront bad ideas with the calm use of facts and logic where possible. Other than his anti-Jewish beliefs my Facebook 'friend' is quite a nice fellow and we share many common interests and beliefs. I do not know why he has these anti-Jewish feelings and beliefs, but when I try to confront him on it he avoids explaining the basis for them. Instead, he posts articles by other people that often contain a certain amount of truth which is then twisted to support an illogical conclusion regarding Jews and Judaism as a whole.

Since he is otherwise a well-spoken and reasonable person, I presume that his anti-Jewish beliefs have more to do with negative feelings that were either inculcated into him at a very early age by his family and friends, or created by some negative experiences he had that involved individual Jews that has since poisoned his views of Jews as a whole. Of course this is all speculations, and I really do not know.

Am I tacitly supporting and approving of Jew-Hatred by not constantly attacking anyone and everyone who express such beliefs? I do not think so. I try to confront bad arguments with good arguments, bad facts with good facts, and lies with truth. At least as best I can. I think there is a real risk that when we respond in a highly emotional, accusative, and angry manner to such irrational and erroneous prejudice we only reinforce it, and perhaps even encourage hatred. I do not want to be part of making a bad situation worse.

I do not believe that everyone who has erroneous prejudices is an evil person. There are a lot of reasons why we can be wrong other than being evil. Furthermore, if every erroneous prejudice means that we are evil, then we are all evil since we all have erroneous prejudices about some people or some things. This makes the term 'evil' meaningless.

The example I use in this article is about Jew-Hatred. This is because I believe that it is the most long-lived and profoundly erroneous prejudice you can find in the world today. There are many other examples out there, but few approach the outrageous falsehoods as those that are leveled against Jews. Furthermore, Jew-Hatred is particularly widespread present among virtually all races, religions, cultures, and nations. The lies are so absurd and unbelievable as to be laughable if they were not so insidiously persistent.

Does anyone really believe that Jews kill non-Jewish children to use their blood in Jewish religious rituals? It is ridiculous but such slurs continue to spread and are believed.

More troubling are those accusations that have a bit of truth behind them: Jews control the world through their 'domination' of business, finance, media, science, and the arts. Clearly, there is a bit of truth here: Jews are more prominent in these endeavors than their percentage in the population would suggest. But it is the insertion of the term 'domination' that turns a simple fact into an outright lie. There are still more non-Jews in these activities than there are Jews so that Jews do not and cannot 'dominate' anyone or anything, and certainly they do not control the world. What about other important areas where Jews show no particular prominence; sports come to mind as well as politics?

I do not want to suggest that those who experience discrimination from other erroneous prejudices suffer less, or that the discrimination experienced is in any manner more justified or acceptable. Only, that Jew-Hatred is the most absurd, and thus should be the easiest to eliminate.

Yet, it persists beyond almost all arguments, facts, and truths.

I suppose this is where the issue of evil comes in.

It is one thing to credulously believe a false statement that someone else says and to even negligently repeat it to others, but it is quite another matter to spread such beliefs when you know they are false and injurious. We cannot spend our entire lives verifying each and every fact, assertion, opinion, or contention, but *we should never knowingly spread lies for the express purpose of injuring and hurting others*. That is evil.

The Origins of Israel: British Colonialism, Zionism, or Arab Stupidity

I am constantly amazed by the lies that are spread by anti-Jewish fanatics. But even more so by the stupidity. In hindsight I am not very enthusiastic about Israel being a Jewish state. I think it was a mistake. Could you find a worse place surrounded by worse people? But Israel does exist as a Jewish state, and I believe this happened because of one and only one thing: Arab stupidity. But for Arab stupidity Israel would never have come into existence. And it would seem that this stupidity is not going away anytime soon.

I suppose what I am trying to say is that reality is very different from what Pro-Palestinians are promoting as the truth. This does not mean that Zionism is correct, nor does it mean that Palestinians should have no rights. It simply means that almost everything that is being said in favor of the Palestinian cause is based on lies. *Unnecessary and counter-productive lies.* And the results of this misleading and outright false narrative has been a tragedy that has needlessly brought about the very opposite of what Palestinians and their supporters have been hoping, or at least claiming, to achieve.

Let us start with the famous Balfour Declaration. Both sides like to over-state the importance of the Balfour Declaration in 1917. It was a vague and ambiguous declaration by a British diplomat that was initially embraced by most parties, but when the details of implementation were laid out objections began to emerge. In the 1920 Geneva Conference to sort out the mess, which was attended by Arab delegates, the original designation of the entire Trans-Jordan territory as a homeland for the Jews was reduced to only the land west of the Jordan River. This included Judea and Samaria (or what is now referred to as the West Bank). The issue of the political nature of the "homeland" was left unresolved. That is, it was not agreed that the "right of return" to a Jewish Homeland would equate to a Jewish State. Only that there would be some kind of "right of return" to the area west of the Jordan River.

Jews had been living continuously in the Holy Land for thousands of years along with Christians, Druze and others, and Jews had been quietly returning for hundreds of years without any real problems. In 1840 the Turkish census found that Jerusalem was 40% Jewish (as was Baghdad and a number of other major Arab cities). However, after the 1920 Geneva Conference confirming the Jewish right to return (not the vague and ambiguous Balfour Declaration), Jews from Europe and other non-Arab nations started to immigrate to the British Mandate west of the Jordan River in greater numbers.

At the same time that all this was taking place the Arabs were growing more and more angry. They were angry about a lot of things, but mostly they were quite rightfully angry at Britain for using them during WWI to defeat the Turks (who were allied with the Germans), making promises of an independent Arab nation in exchange for Arab assistance, and then reneging on the promises and instead dividing up the Middle East between Britain and France.

All this anger led to the creation of two separate fascist movements within the Arab World:

1. Arab Nationalism; a secular ideology, with the goal of uniting all Arabs under one nation, was initially inspired by Italian Fascism (and later turned to Nazism), and

2. The Muslim Brotherhood; an ideology that combined Radical Islam with the political structure and tactics of European fascism.

In the later part of the 1920s both of these Arab fascist movements joined together and began focusing upon hatred for the Jews as a tactic to promote their goals, perhaps inspired by German Nazis. There was violent unrest among the Arabs in the British Mandate with the goal of getting rid of the British, and creating a unified Arab Nation. Some of the unrest focused upon the Jewish communities and there were many attacks upon Jews during this time.

By the early 1930s it was obvious to everyone involved that there was no way for a peaceful implementation of the Balfour Declaration or the 1920 Geneva Conference. It was also the consensus among the Jews living in the region that Zionism had more or less failed. During the 1920s only a few hundred thousand Jews had immigrated to the Promised Land, and in the early 1930s the British blocked any further Jewish immigration while Arabs were allowed to enter Palestine in search of jobs and opportunity. Probably more Arabs immigrated into what is now Israel during the 1930s than Jews during the 1920s.

Without an obvious solution, the British decided to abandon the vague promises of the Balfour Declaration and the 1920 Geneva Conference, and encouraged the establishment of a single independent Arab state covering the British Mandate as long as there were guarantees that Jews and other minorities living in the area would be protected: the nation would be called "Trans-Jordan". The Arabs refused to negotiate with the British or the Jews choosing to rely upon their greater numbers to "drive the Jews into the sea, and turn the water red with their blood" (that was the only option the Arabs ever offered). British diplomatic internal correspondence makes it very clear that they had no interest in creating a Jewish State. Similarly, the Jews living west of the Jordan River were more than willing to accept an Arab dominated "One State Solution" as long as it didn't involve the genocide of the Jews (see the private correspondence of the various Jewish negotiators during the 1930s and 1940s). However, no offer was ever put forward by the Arabs other than promises of genocidal slaughter and murder.

When World War II broke out the Arabs supported the Nazis. The Mufti of Jerusalem became a high ranking SS officer, and Arabs were encouraged to join the SS. They didn't see much action, but they did serve to promote Nazi propaganda in the Middle East and elsewhere. The Jews on the other hand joined with the British and fought with distinction in battles across North Africa against Rommel and the Germans. The hardened veterans of the Jewish Brigade returned to Israel after the war to form the core of what is now the Israel Defense Forces (IDF), and made it possible for Israel to survive the onslaught of Arab armies in 1948.

After the end of World War II the British simply wanted out and handed everything over to the newly formed United Nations in a rather cowardly manner. Again, a peaceful solution was impossible because the Arabs continued to demand the death of all Jews living in the Holy Land.

Now let us look back from 1917 to 1947. The fiction that the Balfour Declaration and the British Mandate created a Jewish state is simply untrue. It was the Arabs who created the Jewish state by refusing to allow those Jews living peacefully in the Holy Land to continue to do so. If the Arabs had simply said, *"Jews living in the Trans-Jordan will not be harmed"* Israel would have never come into existence. The only reason the UN partitioned the area was because of the refusal of the Arabs to even negotiate. In frustration the UN declared that Israel would be made up of small separated indefensible Jewish enclaves, and then walked away convinced that the Jews of Israel would be slaughtered and that there was nothing more they could do to prevent it.

By 1947 there were roughly 700,000 Jews living in the Holy Land, and about 700,000 Arabs. Both sides debate claiming each had larger populations at the time, but if it is more or less it is not more or less by much. Most of the Jews were from communities that dated back before the 1920s (remember only 200,000 Jews actually immigrated to Israel after the Balfour Declaration and immigration was then blocked after the 1930s). Most of the Arabs were immigrants who came during the 1920s and 1930s.

How this small group of Jews withstood the military might of most of the Arab World is another story, but survive they did and the state of Israel was born. However, the survival of the

Jewish State was still doubtful. It received yet more unexpected aid from the Arab World!

Not only did the Arabs create Israel through their stupid barbaric genocidal attitudes, they then increased the population of the newly formed state of Israel from 700,000 Jews to millions by forcing out the Jews from Iraq, Egypt, Libya, Algeria, Lebanon, Yemen, etc., and stealing their property (I think Syria and Morocco are the only countries that did not forcibly expel Jews and seize their property — and in fact when Assad came to power in Syria he went to some lengths to protect the Jewish population although some suggest that his motivation had more to do with holding them hostage). It is thus a total lie when people say that Israeli Jews should just return to Europe. To this day, after 70 years of encouraging European and American Jews to immigrate to Israel, 61% of the current Jewish population of Israel trace their roots from Arab lands. Could Egyptian, Iraqi, Iranian, Libyan, Algerian, Lebanese, Yemeni Jews return to those countries? Will they have their property returned to them?

The biggest problem that the Arabs have: they cannot accept the truth.

They created the state of Israel by their blood-thirsty stupidity. The British did not want a Jewish state. The Jews would have accepted an Arab dominated one state solution such as a Hashemite Kingdom of Trans-Jordan, including all of what is now Israel, the West Bank, and Jordan, if their rights would have been protected. Instead the Arabs decided to commit genocide against the Jews, and then failed.

They then more than doubled the Jewish population of Israel by forcibly ejecting over a million Jews living in the Arab World.

Then they started additional wars they didn't need to fight, and each time got their head handed to them, and each time they lost more and more.

Instead of accepting the Arab refugees from these wars and absorbing them back into their countries, they put them into "refugee" camps where they continue to live in poverty and dependence used as pawns by corrupt and evil men. No other group has remained "refugees" for so long and been abused so thoroughly by their own people.

And to this day, they refuse to even acknowledge that they lost. Or that they made any mistakes! How will they ever learn how to win if they refuse to accept their own defeats?

This is why the Arabs are at such a disadvantage. There seems to be a cultural inability to accept the truth, and to use reason to resolve unpleasant situations. If you are an Arab and you stand up and say, "We have been doing this all wrong, we must change our attitudes, our strategies, and our tactics." that man will be shouted down and rejected, or much worse. Just look at what happened to Sadat! And thus they keep making the same stupid mistakes while refusing to acknowledge them.

Where does that leave us? During the Obama Administration the United Nations, with the unethical connivance of the Obama State Department, issued an edict declaring the pre-1967 boundaries the basis for any future negotiations. In so doing they have locked the poor Palestinians into a future of defeat and destruction. The Israelis will not give up their communities in Jerusalem and the West Bank (research the history of those "settlements" — most of them are built on land that had been Jewish settlements prior to 1948, were set aside by the Jordanians in 1948 into special Royal Trusts preventing any development until they were then "liberated" in 1967), and the Palestinians will have no reason to concede anything now that they have received a huge vote of confidence from the United Nations.

A two state solution was always going to be difficult, but it was very close a few decades ago. Now it is an impossibility. As is the possibility of the Israelis and Palestinians finding a way to live in peace. Only the complete destruction of Israel and the death of all Jews will satisfy the current Palestinian leadership and the deluded and misguided people. Essentially, the United Nations, the Obama Regime, Western Europe, and most of the rest of world have made it possible for the Arabs to return to their old tired and discredited policy: "Drive the Jews into the sea, and turn the water red with their blood!"

To the ever suffering Palestinians I say: "Congratulations on your success in the United Nations, let us see how that works out for you."

A Discouraging Afternoon in Old Town Vienna

During the summer of 2018, I walked into the Old Town of Vienna to check out all the nice things my tourist guide book suggested I should go and see. I had imagined there would be beautiful old buildings, shops, hearty food, and music. Well three out of four is not so bad. Instead of music the Old Town was dominated by roaming bands of discontented LGBTXYZ protesters led by some loud obnoxious hag yelling about how neo-Nazis were oppressing her and others like her, all the while surrounded by bands of police prepared to crush the demonstration if it turned nasty.

It did not turn nasty, at least not nasty enough to justify police interference, and the police seemed terribly bored and irritated. Just like me.

Among the various bands of angry LGBTXYZs were two handsome men walking together hand in hand… stumbling along wearing very uncomfortable women's high heels. I just do not get it. Why????? Each man was very good looking… as a man, but neither would have made a very good looking woman, at least in my opinion. I am not sure if it was the beards, the broad shoulders, masculine facial features, etc. Clearly they were not attracted to each other because they looked like good looking women. They were attracted to each other because they were very good looking men, and I suppose that was what they liked.

What is wrong with that????

I am not the bigot saying that there is something wrong with them. They are the ones! They and others like them are the ones saying that there is something wrong with being a man.

What's wrong with being a man? Can't a gay guy walk around town with his boy friend without having to wear ridiculous and uncomfortable women's clothing???

Just when I thought it could not get any worse a small group of angry lesbians came walking down the street towards me. I noticed that in addition to the lovely rainbow flags they had deposited in various parts of their bodies, they were wearing the same white shirt with the black letters boldly written:

WATCH YOUR MIND!

Well that is some good advice. We certainly would not want anyone using that thing without proper supervision from the proper people. No. Best to show no inclination of thinking; just smile and nod, shuck and jive. Can I say shuck and jive? Probably not.

Vienna is a very nice place. Not incredibly exciting, but that is rather as I like it. But this afternoon was rather discouraging. I hope it is just the mindless reflexive response of the Regressive Left as Austria turns away from the foolishness of Political Correctness. I hope.

A response to a proposition regarding Basic Jobs vs Basic Income

This is a response to a very interesting *article by Simon Sarris, 'Why Basic Jobs Are Better That Basic Incomes'* about how the benefits of a Universal Jobs Program would be better than a Universal Basic Income at addressing the possibility of mass unemployment in the future. *You should go and read it.*

People are talking a lot about Universal Basic Incomes because they are imagining a world where people will become obsolete. A world that is filled with superfluous unemployable people who must be fed. The author suggests that UBI is the favorite solution to imagine because the world is filled with people who don't like to think very much. He offers an alternative: Universal Jobs Programs.

I think the first proposition, that people will become superfluous and unemployable, is a flawed one. Yes, AI and robots will make many career choices obsolete and put people out of work, but that doesn't mean people will become unnecessary — or in other words completely lose all economic utility. AI and robots will increase human productivity which means that we will produce more per person than before. This does not necessarily lead to mass unemployment. We have historically failed to imagine how the future will be if and when the world becomes more productive. This has been a characteristic of human thought for centuries — we imagine that progress will only bring disaster. We fail to understand how added production will never outstrip the limitless needs and wants of human desire. In fact I think it is fair to say that the more you give people the more they want. It is an innate aspect of human psychology. So I think the issue of chronic unemployment may be no more valid now with the prospect of AI and robots than when the steam engine, the cotton gin, the railroads, and the automobile were all introduced with calls of alarm that mule drivers, hand weavers, pony express riders, and horse drawn wagoneers were losing their jobs.

If I am right, and AI and robots do not make human workers superfluous so much as make them much more productive, that does not mean these changes will be entirely beneficial. During the last 500 years the Age of Discovery, the Industrial Age, and now the Silicon Age have brought about unprecedented increases in prosperity on every measurable scale. It has also increased the numbers of people who get lost and are left behind. As the ground underneath us tectonically erupts with the frenetic technological advances which create prosperity and opportunity for most people, there have been others that fall through the cracks. These people who are left behind are confused and abandoned. There is no reason to believe this problem will not persist in the future.

This is because the changes that have taken place in the Modern World are much more profound than those changes during ancient times. For thousands of years the poor have been a natural part of human culture. They were in fact the norm. Just a part of a static society which did not dramatically change over time. From the beginnings of agriculture thousands of years ago to the feudal system of the medieval times little really changed in everyday lives. The adoption of bronze simply meant fewer stone tools, and the adoption of iron meant fewer stone and bronze tools. Swords got sharper, bowls more attractive, plows became slightly more efficient, etc. These changes were not like the revolutionary changes that have taken place in the modern world with the introduction of powered engines and computer sciences. The technological advances of the ancient world did not leave vast sections of the population behind. Today's advanced technology does just that.

Personally I am against both Universal Jobs Programs and Universal Basic Income to address the possibility of mass unemployment since, again, I think these solutions are based upon the false premise that there will in fact be mass unemployment. I suspect that rather than mass unemployment we will instead face the very real and difficult challenge of how to help the small but significant portion of the population falling through the cracks.

The fact that this situation is not new does not make it any less difficult to address. It is clear that we need some way to take care of those chronically lost and helpless, and also those that simply need a helping hand in the painful adjustment caused by sudden and unexpected changes. We have such welfare programs today. Which programs work best?

We have already experimented with Basic Income programs (just not Universal programs), and most of these efforts have resulted in societal disasters too numerous to describe here. Just giving people money does not seem to work. We have also experimented with Jobs Programs (again just not Universal) and have seen much better results. It is true that getting the government involved in providing or guaranteeing jobs results in chronic examples of incompetence, waste, and corruption. Furthermore, during the 20th century we have seen many communists countries create monumental projects that have often resulted in a mass destruction. Getting the government involved in giant monumental construction programs increases the risk of giant monumental failures. However, although the examples of failure are sadly obvious, there are ways of limiting these negatives while providing the basic goal of gainful employment and income to those in need. An example of a successful modern welfare program that does just that is the US Earned Income Tax Credit which rewards poor families who work by lifting them out of poverty with a reverse income tax scheme; perhaps this is even a combination of the Jobs and Income approach.

As the author of the above article points out providing Jobs is always better than just providing Money, and he addresses the problems of how to do so. I like his ideas. Instead of creating massive centralized bureaucracies to manage these problems, he suggest decentralizing the process by giving local 'townhalls' the ability to figure out for themselves what and how to best deal with their local problems.

I also like his idea of encouraging a return to the soil and the manual trades that may have been eliminated in the past and may be completely lost in the future. Just because a giant factory run by an AI and using robots makes more beer (or whatever...) at a lower price does not mean we as a society have to choose that alternative. Instead we can choose to encourage craftsmen to continue to pursue their professions. We may not even need to have the government subsidize such activities so much as get the government out of the way so that people are better able to do what they like with what they have in their homes, yards, and garages. This vision involves a return to cottage industries of the past but with a much more humane and dignified approach.

Those people in trades made superfluous by technology may need help to find another trade, but the people themselves need not become superfluous. However, if we are going to be successful in this decentralized vision where people pursue local agriculture and manual trades we will need to change how we think about our lives.

An example: Our food is much more sanitary, safe, and appealing today than it was in the past — no flecks of dirt or the occasional bug. We will need to adjust our expectation if we are going to start buying food from our neighbors rather than from large multi-national corporations with the latest technology. It will not be long before these large corporations will be able to produce the most sanitary and appealing foods with robots doing everything from planting, growing, picking, and processing the crops, and then preparing, packaging, and delivering the food in nice shiny containers ready to be served in our homes. Some people may see the organic gardens grown by our neighbors as horrifically outdated, inconvenient, and perhaps even dangerous.

The same issue may arise in almost everything. Would you prefer to go to the IKEA website of the future and order your furniture delivered and assembled to your house the next day by a sole workman (perhaps not even that) using robots to assemble and place the furniture, or would you prefer to go to a local craftsman who spent years learning his trade, and will spend days if not months making your furniture using traditional tools and methods? Both futures have their trade offs.

Predicting the future is always a difficult and often thankless task, but it seems clear that one aspect of modern progress will continue — people are going to fall through the cracks as society as a whole advances. We have already experimented with the idea of throwing money at these problems, and we have already discovered that the societal costs are much greater than the benefits. If we end up having this problem of mass unemployment caused by technological progress or just a significant portion of the population falling through the cracks, let us look to Jobs as a better solution.

What is the democratization process?

Democratization (or democratisation) is the transition to a more democratic political regime, including substantive political changes moving in a democratic direction. It may be the transition from an authoritarian regime to a full democracy, a transition from an authoritarian political system to a semi-democracy or transition from a semi-authoritarian political system to a democratic political system. (Wikepedia)

Thanks Wikipedia!

But I don't really like this. It misses the important issues of HOW and WHAT. How do you move from authoritarian government to 'democratic' self-rule, and what does 'democracy' mean?

For most situations 'democratization' seems to involve little more than some sort of popular uprising involving protests, peaceful or violent, followed by a hasty election that replaces the unpopular regime with a somewhat more popular regime. Other than the election little changes.

If all you are doing is voting for your dictator I do not believe you live in a democracy. Democracy should involve self-rule.

Self-rule requires institutions that develop at the grass roots that give the people real authority in how they live their lives. Few countries have these grass roots institutions and even less have a population ready to take control of their government operations.

If you live in a country where all the decisions of government are made in the capital by elites of one type or another, then you do not live in a democracy.

Examples of grass roots institutions that lead to and indicate successful self-rule: local school districts run by parents and neighbors; police departments controlled by elected officials selected by the local voters; public works departments and public utilities that are controlled by the local people who receive the benefits; etc.

These are not easy to develop. In most countries if you suddenly devolve the authority of the central government down to the local level corruption would increase rather than decrease. That is because the people themselves are not ready for democracy. It is not an easy thing to go from obedient slave to that of a civic minded citizen of your community. A citizen that is equal among his or her peers, and able to resist the temptations of corruption and abuse of power. Do most people even understand what that means? From my travels around the world I don't think they do.

If you hand most local communities control of their local government operations, instead of committee meetings filled with local citizens voicing their ideas and grievances and then deciding among themselves the best way to solve problems and improving things, a local criminal cabal would develop that would just steal the office supplies and start extorting money from their neighbors.

Also, in addition to not being ready or fit for self-rule, most people do not even want it. Freedom involves a lot of responsibility and can be a very heavy burden. Do you and your neighbors really want the burden of running the local school district? Do you have the confidence and experience to do so? Wouldn't it be better to have all that managed by people in the central government who have been trained to do just that in prestigious colleges and universities?

People like the idea of Freedom! They don't like the burden and responsibilities that come with it.

Love vs Utility

As I become older I have discovered a painful truth: very few people love or care for me. When I was young I expected to be surrounded by people who would love me, but as I approach the age of 55 I realize that those people do not exist. I find this disappointing. Not only did I expect love and affection as I approach my elder years, but I believed I was entitled to it. That is because I gave my love and affection freely only to discover it was not reciprocated, at least not to the degree that I expected.

For a long time I denied that this was the case. It was not true! They do love me, but they just do not know how to show it! This made me a little sad, but I deluded myself into believing that it would get better if I would just provide more love and attention. Needless to say, that did not improve anything, but only made me more disappointed, and much worse: I became angry, frustrated, and resentful. How dare you! Damn it, I am entitled to your love!

Instead of being surrounded by a loving family, I find myself totally alone. I have discovered that the world is filled with people who do not love or care about me, and, furthermore, that those people who I expected to love me are at best indifferent. This realization was and still is incredibly painful. Much of the initial pain has since subsided. The reality has set in. Life goes on. At least that is what I tell myself.

Over time I realized the foolishness of all this. Why should I be angry and frustrated by the fact that I was not loved? Why should I believe I am entitled to love and affection? How was anger and frustration going to change anything, or make my life better? Simply stated it won't. It will only make me bitter and resentful. Being alone and disappointed is bad enough, but being bitter, angry, and lonely is something much worse.

Now you may be thinking at this point, "What a sad and pathetic, and even cynical guy!" If you are prone to sentimentality, you may even feel a bit of sympathy for me. I would ask you to hold back on those feelings for a bit, and instead think about the possibility that we are all in the same situation. You see, I would suggest that there is a big difference between love and utility, and that most of our disappointment and frustration comes from confusing the two.

Wikipedia defines love broadly as:

> *"...a range of strong and positive emotional and mental states, from the most sublime virtue or good habit, the deepest interpersonal affection and to the simplest pleasure. An example of this range of meanings is that the love of a mother differs from the love of a spouse, which differs from the love of food. Most commonly, love refers to a feeling of strong attraction and emotional attachment."*

Your utility on the other hand has to do with what you can do for someone else. Someone may sincerely like and enjoy what you do for them without necessarily loving you. There is nothing wrong with this. You may provide them with food and shelter, comfort and charm, entertainment, employment, or other valuable and important things in their lives. Respect and appreciation is valuable but are not necessarily love.

Perhaps the above definition of 'love' should be refined. It is too broad. According to this definition people can love all sorts of things: parents, spouses, children, sports teams, lasagna, beer, etc. I would suggest that this use of the word 'love' is overly inclusive and encompasses much that is merely appreciation of utility. For love to have significance it must be something more. You really do not love that bottle of wine, you just really like it. You find it pleasurable to drink… in fact you may find it so pleasurable that you enjoy just possessing it since owning it reminds you of the satisfaction that comes from actually enjoying it with a meal. There is nothing wrong with this but it is not love.

I would suggest that love is something much more. Love is the appreciation of someone or something that goes beyond utility, and is in fact an appreciation of something more innate and intrinsic.

If that bottle of wine goes sour will you still love it? What if it is not only unfit to drink, but it smells bad? Will you keep it around even though you no longer want to drink it, and you find its presence mildly offensive?

"Surely," you say, "that is all fine and good when considering something like a bottle of wine, but it cannot apply to people!"

I believe there is no real difference between the two. At least for most people. I think most people are sincerely and honestly confused about their own feelings for others as well as for the feelings of others towards them. It is only natural. All our lives we are told 'love' is the most important thing without anyone properly explaining the true nature of love.

Our children surely love us! When our children are young they are dependent upon us. For years we selflessly feed them, protect them, entertain them, and educate them; in short we provide for their every want and need to the extent of our ability. If we fail to so provide for them they may not properly develop, and in fact may die. As a result when we walk into the room they welcome us with smiles, hugs, and adoration. If that is not love what is?

Is a child's sincere and honest appreciation of the value of what parents provide really love? Or is it just the recognition of the immediate utility that is being provided?

As a parent I can only say that you discover this only when your children become independent and no longer need you. When they are no longer dependent upon you and you are no longer useful to them will they still welcome your presence with affection and devotion? Will they call you to ask how you are doing? Will they worry about your health and well-being? Or will you discover that they only call when they need something from you? Or perhaps even worse; they only call with resentment when their conscience requires them to do so?

Each case is different. Perhaps you can honestly answer yes to the above questions, and that you are correct in believing that your children love you. If so then you are blessed. I am happy for you. For many parents there will be an unpleasant discovery that when your children grow up and are less dependent upon you, which is a good thing — it means you have done your job, they will become more distant and uncaring. If you are honest with yourself you will realize they do no love you. They do not appreciate you for anything more than what you can do for them, and as time passes so does your usefulness. I suppose that is why most people are not very honest with themselves; they prefer the comfort of believing lies.

The same analysis can be performed regarding spouses, and I suspect in most cases love is being confused with utility. When one or both spouses realize this fact, that their spouse does not love them but at best tolerates them for their usefulness, the marriage usually is over whether or not it ends in divorce. There may yet be enough mutual respect and appreciation for the relationship to continue, but from my experience the realization that your spouse does not love you results in anger and resentment which is not conducive to a peaceful and productive relationship.

What of friends? Surely friends love you! You are not taking care of them, they do not depend upon you, you owe them no duty or obligation. They don't have to put up with your crap! They must love you. Perhaps. Or perhaps they simply enjoy your company, you distract them from their own troubles and concerns, or you provide them with entertainment. Perhaps you just give them a sense of human contact, a brief escape from their loneliness.

Like that sour bottle of wine, the only time you learn if someone really loves you is when you are not only without utility, but your presence becomes an annoying burden. It is only then, when you are at your worst, when you are most vulnerable, and you are least useful that you will discover who loves you and appreciates you for who you are rather than what you can do for them. For most people this is going to be a very unpleasant revelation.

"Ok," you say, "So what am I supposed to do about it? Sit around moping and being sad all the time?"

I would suggest that is not a healthy attitude to have, and it certainly is not a good solution. I suggest that instead of 'moping' about and feeling sorry for yourself you accept reality and move on. If someone appreciates you for what you can do for them, that is not the worst thing in the world. Seek out those people, and enjoy their company… at least while it lasts. Don't pretend that you are anything more to them, nor that they are anything more to you. This may seem cold and heartless, and it may feel more comfortable to delude yourself into believing that utility is really love, but if and when the truth is ever revealed to you it is going to be very painful. Pain drives people to stupidity and foolishness. Wisdom would suggest that you accept those things which you cannot change as gracefully as possible.

As for love, you may be blessed with people who sincerely value you for who you are instead of what you can do for them. Perhaps those relationships that were initially based only upon mutual self-interest and respect will grow into something deeper and more meaningful. If so treasure those people. Nurture them and love them back if you can.

The Failure of Modern Western Democracy

In my humble opinion the problem with the current system in the USA, and also Western Europe, is the introduction of too much democracy at the state and national level, and too little at the local level. Mencken once said, "Democracy is the theory that the common people know what they want, and deserve to get it good and hard."

In 1910 the first US state used the primary system, and within a few years almost all states used them for both the Democrats and the Republicans. This is not part of the Constitution or the law in any way. It is just the way that the states and the two largest political parties decided to select their candidates.

Before the primary system, the state parties would elect representatives to go to the national convention, and those representatives would smoke a lot of cigars and drink a lot of whiskey and then they would decide upon who would win the nomination among themselves. Only after the national conventions were finished did the national elections begin. Was this system democratic at the party level? Most certainly not. But the results were far better than what we see today.

The USA was designed to be a representative republic not a direct democracy. As such the people should not control the state and national governments, but instead they vote for local leaders who will represent them at the state and national level. If those local leaders do a good job they get re-elected. At least that is how it was initially intended to work, and it seemed to work quite well for over a hundred years.

I think democracy works at the local level, but not at the national level of a country like the USA, or even for most of the larger states. People do not have enough information or experience to make intelligent and wise decisions about anything other than what is effecting them on an individual, family, and community level. They are also too vulnerable to marketing and propaganda beyond the local level.

Where most Western 'democracies' fail is not giving the people control at the local levels, and thus we end up with a population with zero experience in managing their own local affairs, no knowledge of the issues that need to be considered at state and national level, and the voters are thus extremely vulnerable to dishonest marketing that results in the very worst and most incompetent people getting elected to important state and national offices.

Note that not ALL leaders are incompetent, just the ones we choose after being sold lies and propaganda by some of the most dishonest and evil people who have ever claimed to be journalists.

By giving people more democracy at the state and national level while removing their democracy at the local level we end up with the worst case scenario: a nation run by a dishonest cabal of corrupt politicians, unscrupulous big businesses, and an evil priesthood of pseudo-journalists covering for the incompetence and cupidity of the first two.

Instead I favor direct democracy on the local level, and representative government on the state and local levels. This system makes it possible to better manage government at all levels and counters the dangerous dictatorial oligarchic tendencies of those who are selected at the state and national.

It is here that Europe fails, and the USA is following in those same bungling fascist footsteps.

Western 'democracies' pretend to allow democracy, but it is just a farce… you don't really get to decide what happens, but only which side of the same political coin you get to vote for. You only get to choose which brand of cigarettes or beer you want to smoke or drink. Whichever one you choose is fine since the same people make them all, and they all work together hand in hand to protect the status quo giving them ultimate control over everything. If that is what you call 'democracy' then I can do without it.

Sadly, on the local level instead of the people deciding how to live their lives, everything is controlled by inept greedy dishonest 'experts' in the capital cities who all go to the same schools, live in the same neighborhoods, go to the same parties, eat at the same restaurants, etc. — and are never held accountable.

Democracy at the local level gets people familiar with how to managing their own affairs, and at the same time wisely choose those local leaders who go on to represent them in state and national government. The state and national leaders are held accountable by a population which is familiar with the workings of government. Without this local democracy the people become foolish and greedy, and eager for the lies coming from an intolerable alliance of useless political leaders, rapacious oligarchic big businesses, and propagandists pretending to be journalists.

If you want 'democracy' to work, we need to restore or install it at the local level, and remove it from the state and national level to be replaced by an accountable representative republican system.

The Five Stages of Grief

(Written in 2017)

I have been asking myself, "Why won't patriotic and knowledgeable Americans do anything useful in the face of a chronic situation?" I have spoken to so many people about this and I am beyond frustration. They know there is something very wrong with America, but all they do is talk and put their faith in corrupt politicians and a corrupt system. The latest has been Donald Trump. Worried conservatives gave him their blind faith:

- He is Going to Make America Great Again!

- He is Going to Drain the Swamp!

- He is Going to Restore Justice and Constitutional Law Back to the USA!

Well so far that has turned out to be a great disappointment, at least to me. He has not drained the swamp, has not prosecuted obvious criminal behavior, he has not even removed the corrupt people from high positions in government that was his right as a new president by appointing his own choices. I am trying to be diplomatic when I approach current and former Trump supporters on the subject: what if he is yet another in a long line of politicians who have let us down — what do we do?

I see most doing the same old things — looking for a hero/messiah to save the day — but some are starting to show progress. Very slowly. These are smart people! Why is this taking so long?

> *I then realized you cannot reason with people in mourning. They are not suffering from a lack of understanding… they are grieving.*

Then I remembered the <u>Five Stages of Grief</u>. For that is what is really going on. People have watched in shock as everything they loved about the USA has been destroyed, and every institution they were raised to admire and respect has betrayed them. Something precious just up and died. This is not a time for reason, but a time for empathy.

The Five Stages of Grief:

1. Denial – avoidance, confusion, fear —   it is very common for people to initially deny the event.

2. Anger – people that are grieving often become upset and irritated over the situation — they seek a target to blame.

3. Bargaining – often defined by magical thinking — calling out to the universe (or some hero type figure) to fix the problem, reverse the disaster, or just make the pain go away.

4. Depression – depression often takes some time to set it — there is a lot of shock and other emotions to process

first — depression due to grief usually appears when a sense of finality is realized.

5. Acceptance – the person is no longer looking to recover what they have lost — they are ready to move on.

I think most American conservatives are somewhere between Denial and Anger. They recognized that there is/was something very wrong, and they are angry that their country has been taken from them. They blamed Obama, Clinton, etc., and voted for Trump to fix it. Some now realize that Donald Trump may just be a fraud, or even if he really is who he claims to be he is just one man fighting against a hopelessly corrupt system. No one is doing anything to fix anything… nor will they. In their anger and confusion they pour their faith into Trump. Now they will either stay in Denial and Anger — and are thus hopeless cases — or they will move past Anger to Bargaining (hoping that some magical force or hero will make the world right — Jesus, Buddha, Mr. T…). Perhaps this blind faith in Trump is part of the Bargaining stage? Those people are making progress. How to get them past Bargaining???? I don't know. But only those who are past Bargaining are ready to act.

As I look back on my own progression through Grief I realize that I am somewhere between Depression and Acceptance. And I have been at it for twenty years. It was five years ago after the American People voted to re-elect Obama that I finally realized there was no hope for the USA. I gave up on Bargaining for something unimaginable to come along and reignite the American Spirit of Liberty. It was only then that I was able to move on. It was only then that I committed to getting out while I could. I am very glad I did. I am still terribly sad about what has happened to my country, and I am sad that my children will not have what I grew up with, but I am finally actively working to make things better for myself and those I can help. I am creating a new life that is much better for my family.

I am going to try to be patient with others who are perhaps not as far along the stages of grief as I am. But I am also going to look at people with an eye towards what stage they are on. Whether there is any chance they will ever make any progress past Denial and Anger. For most I fear any progress they make will be too late for them and everyone else around them.

The Ideologies of ANTIFA and BLM in a Nutshell

Both ANTIFA and BLM have been in the news a lot lately, but very few people know what they are really about. I thought I would offer up this brief explanation.

Both ANTIFA and BLM are inspired by Leftwing Marxist teachings but they are not identical. ANTIFA is a 'traditional' Stalinist/Leninist Marxist revolutionary movement that seeks to create a Utopian Socialist state by creating a conflict between the working class and the capitalists through a class war. BLM is a Neo-Marxist revolutionary movement that seeks to create a Utopian socialist inspired world by creating multiple cleavages between races, ethnic groups, religions, and economic and cultural backgrounds through a race war. Both organizations seem similar in that they believe that for their Utopian visions of the future to take place the current system must be shattered and destroyed so that a new age of equality can begin.

The differences between ANTIFA and BLM are subtle but they are not insignificant.

Don't be terribly surprised when you talk to your friends in ANTIFA and BLM and they do not share the above described ideological beliefs. Most Marxist movements do not spend a lot of time on ideological issues other than creating a basic belief system among followers that is inspirational and actionable. Most of the ANTIFA and BLM 'activists' you meet in the street know very little about their own movements. And that is how the leaders want it to stay.

Perhaps you would like to know more about the historical rise of these movements and more importantly the ideological underpinnings of both ANTIFA and BLM. I have tried to explain these things to people in the past only to see their eye's glaze over. Most people are not interested in any of this stuff. Pity, I find it fascinating. I shall not attempt that here. If you are really interested feel free to do your own research!

Perhaps you don't trust me — after all your friends in ANTIFA are talking about creating an anarchic state where people are free to do what they want when they want as they want with no one from the top telling anyone what to do, and your friends in BLM are telling you that its all about Black Lives and restitution and reparation of past wrongs. None of this Marxist stuff! Well again, feel free to go investigate on your own. Its all open and available for anyone who is curious enough to explore.

More pointedly you may suggest that the differences between ANTIFA and BLM that I described above are not really that important. This is something I will address.

Again, ANTIFA is based upon a traditional ideology of Stalinist/Leninist Marxism. BLM is based upon a more recent school of thought sometimes referred to as Neo-Marxism. Why these subtle differences are significant is because they create very different movements with very different goals and potential outcomes.

ANTIFA relies upon the old Marxist tactic of revolution through class warfare. After the revolution the means of production as well as the management of the state will be vested in the Dictatorship of the Proletariat insuring a fair and equitable future based upon science and progress!

BLM is based upon something different. Neo-Marxism grew out of the failures of traditional Marxist revolutions. Neo-Marxists acknowledge the past failures of Marxism but still believe in the underlying principals. Neo-Marxists declare that class warfare was a failure because it was not a strong enough division to base a societal revolution upon. Historically most of the working class ended up opposing the Communist Revolution and either actively supported the counter-revolution or simply refused to take sides. As such the Neo-Marxists have decided that there needs to be a more powerful basis to split society apart; race, ethnicity, religious beliefs, etc. are the cracks that allow them to divide and conquer. BLM in particular is based upon starting and winning a race war.

Thus the two movements believe in very different tactics regarding the Revolution.

What makes the two movements even more different is their ultimate goals which are not compatible. ANTIFA sees the creation of a traditional Communist State run by the Party on egalitarian grounds without any future racial, ethnic, religious or other differences between peoples. BLM sees a very different world where the past oppressors are punished, preferably to extinction, and the new world will based upon those very racial, ethnic, and religious differences that are supposed to be eliminated in traditional Marxist ideology.

If ANTIFA gets what it wants the world will become a cool version of the Soviet Union with fewer tanks and all the comrades having the same high quality cellphone, Universal Basic Income, a 30 hour work week for those so inclined to work, etc. If BLM gets what it wants we are going to see a massive Cambodian style Killing Fields where anyone identified as being a member of an 'oppressive' race, ethnicity, religion, etc. will be liquidated to make room for those righteous few who remain. Remember, Pol Pot was one of the early Neo-Marxists.

Of the two groups ANTIFA is the least dangerous. They are not very well organized, their ideology is based upon a discredited Communist dogma, and their tactics are crude and unlikely to succeed. BLM on the other hand is very well organized, is very well funded, its core ideology is reprehensible but its public facade has the potential to be attractive to the uninformed, and their tactics are much more subtle and effective.

So pick your poison!

A response to a video from Russel Brand

In response to the YouTube video created by Russel Brand 18 July 2021, entitled 'Thought Amazon Couldn't Sink Any Lower?? THINK AGAIN!!!'.

My only problem here is semantics… what I consider the misuse of the term 'Capitalism'. The proper understanding of the meaning of words is important in order to avoid confusion.

Capitalism is not what you are describing in this video. Capitalism is simply a set of rules that under ideal circumstances creates a fair and free system for people to work and compete within. Of course there are never true ideal circumstances, but Capitalism comes closest to liberating the creative spirit and humanity of the individual.

I think what you are justly criticizing is closer to Oligarchic Fascism or Corporate Fascism (or just Corporatism) which grew out of classic Marxism/Socialism and is the opposite of Capitalism. Corporatism was designed to unify the 'means of production' under government control by imagining/creating distinct autonomous classes which are then integrated into the state. You have the investor class, the manager class, and the workers all separate but equal under the firm guidance of the government apparatus. However, even in the 19th and early 20th centuries these separate classes were largely contrivances, and now they are wholly artificial having to be maintained by the heavy hand of authoritarianism in order to prop up an unnatural system. Marxism on the other hand seeks to wholly eliminate such classes and in so doing people become dehumanized cogs in a grand authoritarian scheme.

Corporatism is not Capitalism. Nor is it even a natural reality… at least not a reality as it would exist in a non-contrived and artificial system. Does a worker who saves some money to invest cease being a worker because he is now also an investor? And if the worker/investor decides to invest his savings into his own business rather than another business, does he cease acting as a worker/investor and instead becomes a manager? These separate classes, if they were ever historically real, were artificially imposed by a rigid social system that needed or needs to keep people in certain roles in order to preserve the authority of the rulers.

By using the term Capitalism to describe Corporatism you encourage the false dichotomy of Left vs Right (Socialism vs Capitalism). You say this is not your intention, and I believe you, but it is still a risk of misusing such inappropriate semantics.

Corporatism is not Capitalism. It is instead a soft form of Socialism. Instead of wholly destroying the various roles that people have within the 'means of production' under Socialism, and thus wholly destroying the humanity of the people involved, Corporatism gives people a contrived community role within the system while depriving them of their individual agency.

Under the ideal Capitalist system the individual would be free to participate in whatever role he chose at a given place and time. Since not everyone is identical there will of course be inequalities of outcome. But these inequalities of outcome would result from the natural interaction of free and independent people making their own choices, and not imposed upon people by a rigid authoritarian system that deprives individuals of their humanity and agency.

Long Live the Revolution!

(This article was written in September of 2020.)

This summer's Marxist revolution involving BLM and ANTIFA (if you are interested in my opinion regarding the true nature of BLM and ANTIFA see the essay above: The Ideologies of ANTIFA and BLM in a Nutshell) is part of an ongoing over-reaction to The Donald (or Orange Man Bad if you prefer) by the Leftist Elites (or the The Swamp or the Deep State — take your pick).

And it may very well be the undoing of them. But don't start celebrating just yet. It may be the undoing of the rest of us as well.

During the last 50 to 70 years, the Marxists inside the USA have accomplished a non-violent 'Long March through the Institutions' and came out in control of the universities, the media (news and entertainment), the national and state government bureaucracies, big businesses, and they have gained effective control of the Democratic Party and a great deal of influence in the Republican Party. They are still a minority, but they control all the political tools of society. With Obama they took control of the national law enforcement and military hierarchy. If you were going to execute a coup those would be the levers of power you would want to seize control over. All the while the rest of us complained ineffectually and did nothing.

Then Trump was elected when he was supposed to lose to the Anointed One. The Elites were shocked.

How did it happen?

Unfortunately for the Elites they really did not make any sincere effort to answer that question. If they had seriously sought an answer they would have concluded that the election of Trump was more of an opposition vote against a particularly vile candidate and perhaps a vague knee-jerk reaction against a globalist set of policies that were impoverishing the working class. Instead of reacting calmly to to the setback… working to co-opt the inexperienced and unprepared Trump in an effort to neutralize him, they responded in a rather hysterical manner opposing him at all levels and seeking to remove him.

Instead of treating Trump as an anomaly caused by their over-reaching and heavy handedness — an anomaly that would most likely have passed as the restive masses who elected him resumed their supine positions after having a few bones thrown their way — our Elites decided to threaten their own hard won victories in the Long March and the Culture Wars by fomenting a real revolution using the violent, and in their eyes gullible fools, in BLM and ANTIFA in a final effort to topple Trump and restore themselves to power.

All they had to do was outlast Trump — another 4 years at worst — and then they would have been back in power. But it turned out they were a bunch of nervous Nellies and they couldn't wait that long.

Starting a real revolution is very dangerous. First of all the revolutionary genie may not want to go back into the bottle after the Master's goals have been achieved, and there is a possibility that the obvious excesses that take place during a revolution will result in a counter-revolution that the Elites will not be able to suppress.

We will see if the American Sheeple have any fight left in them. And more importantly if there is any leadership capable of taking control of a counter-revolution and leading it effectively. My guess is NO. So the Swamp has that going for them.

As for what happens to the revolutionary genies of BLM and ANTIFA, that will be an interesting thing to watch. But probably not a pleasant thing. Leading up to the Russian Revolution the Bolsheviks were supported by an odd mixture of German military intelligence seeking to undermine the Russian war effort during WWI, and 'Elite' elements within the Russian government, military and intelligence services, and Russian cultural intelligentsia that wanted to modernize Russia at any cost. These Elites thought the radical Bolsheviks, along with other revolutionary movements, would be ideal tools to use to topple the government… and that these revolutionary movements would then be very easy to dispose of once the Elites were in power. That didn't quite work out as they planned.

I suspect BLM and ANTIFA may prove to be similarly resilient, and will ignore the calls by the Elites to go home after they have served their intended purpose. If they follow the historical course of most such revolutions there will be a brief but very nasty internal purge that will leave only one operating revolutionary movement standing. Then the surviving group will begin consolidating power by turning against the very Elites that brought them into existence, and destroying any other groups that might stand in their way.

We will see. A lot depends upon the result of this election. Or not.

PS: Some of you may take issue with my dismissive and less than optimistic view of the rise of a successful counter-revolution. A counter-revolution needs leadership. There is no such leadership in the USA. At best such a counter-revolution could evolve on a regional basis and thus could be attacked and eliminated piecemeal — or just ignored and allowed to putter about until the revolutionaries decided they were powerful enough to force them back into the 'Union'. "But surely you are under-estimating the influence of Trump! He won't let the country devolve into a Marxist Revolution!" He already has. Roughly half of the country is now controlled by Marxists in one way or another — California, Oregon, Washington, Minnesota, Wisconsin, Illinois, New York, etc (I am sure I am missing some). As described above the 'Long March through the Institutions' have effectively given control over most of the national political infrastructure to the Leftist Elites. Trump is not a leader of the future. He is the last gasp of a dead regime — the national government fell to the Marxists over a decade ago. Trump is an anachronistic hold over from the 'ancien regime' — an anomaly that never represented a viable governing force within the national apparatus. At the national level Trump is surrounded by powerful enemies that have and will continue to oppose anything he tries to do. One step out of line and he will be eliminated. I suspect trying to lead a counter-revolution would be suicide for him and his family. That is too much to expect of anyone.

The only hope America has is that the Elites turn out to be so incompetent and the revolutionaries so irrational as to begin fighting among themselves before actually obtaining a complete victory, giving the rest of us an opportunity to step up and form a viable alternative. Hope costs nothing, but is not a good strategy. Again, we will see what happens next.

The Psychology of Freedom… or Not Giving a Shit?

In the past I have spent a great deal of thought and energy in pointless attempts to create a group of like minded people who want to be free, and then working together to try to achieve our mutual goals.

I now realize that to be free you have to not really give a shit about too much of anything. I am no longer looking for that perfect place where 'WE' can all be free together! I now realize that most people don't really want freedom or privacy or yada yada yada. Its just the noise that some sheep make while jabbering. Most people like being in the warm and comforting embrace of tyranny. I have given up on finding a 'home' that I can share with fellow freedom lovers. That animal is far too rare to come across on a regular basis. Nor am I looking for an ideal place where I can settle down. No, now I am just looking for places where I can be free to do what I want on my own without too much interference from others.

In 2015 I left the good ole USS of A for sunny Israel. I was pursuing my dream of returning to Israel (in both meanings of the term – as a 'returning' Jew and as someone who visited Israel in the late 1980s and really liked it). I went to Israel expecting to be at 'home'.

That feeling lasted about a month, and then I started getting pissed. What really pissed me off, and what made it impossible for me to live happily there, was the false expectation on my part that I would be accepted as an Israeli. When I realized that I would never be accepted as an Israeli no matter what I did (learn Hebrew, happily swallow the shit Israelis have to put up with, repeat the dumb ass shit that Israelis tell each other, etc.) – that I would always be a profoundly distrusted Oleh (Hebrew for immigrant) – I completely lost interest. My Hebrew actually got worse while I was there. My subconscious mind went out of its way to remove it my from skull.

Now I don't really give a shit about any of that anymore. At least that is what I tell myself.

I ended up leaving Israel for a one month vacation to the Republic of Georgia... and I never went back. I bought a nice house in an old neighborhood in Tbilisi, and thought I had found 'home'. For the first 2 years everything was going so great that I actually bought into all the bullshit that they were dishing out about Georgia; that it was a free market paradise, that the people really liked foreigners, that I had found a place where I could be at home! Not only that, but I bought into the bullshit that I was some sort of genius or prophet! What an idiot I was.

About 3 years ago everything started going south in Georgia. The Georgians went from being insanely pro-foreigner to being insanely anti-foreigner. I should have picked up on the 'insane' part earlier. Oh well. I managed to pick up on it early enough to divest myself of most of my very unwise investments in the country, at a substantial profit, and now I just have some real property there which is not even worth trying to sell.

Real property that I have not been able to see since January of 2020. I was visiting the USSA on some personal business, and then the BeerBug Lockdowns trapped me there. No more flights to Georgia for me! I stayed in the USSA as long as I could, pretending to be happy, but the place just gets under my skin like a bad rash.

Right now I am in Mexico, and mostly I am enjoying myself. I feel free here. More free than most Mexicans I suspect. You can go on and on about this or that bad news about Mexico, but I don't give a shit. Not only do I not care about what happens here, other than to the point that it directly effects me, I don't even understand most of what they are saying. Its rather liberating!

I tried to get to that point in the USSA – just don't give a shit – do whatever I want regardless of what the assholes tell me to do – but I can't do it. I look around at my country and it makes me want to weep.

No matter how fucked up Mexico or Georgia or wherever may be I just don't give a shit. Its good for me now and that's good enough. If I found out that Mexico was no longer good for me, I would be on the next airplane out without a second thought. No matter how hard I try with the USSA I just cannot do that.

I have no delusions anymore that I am going to find some perfect place. Nor do I have any belief that I will find other people who share my desires and beliefs. Everyplace you go is going to be screwed up more or less, and everyone I meet is a sheep... more or less. Now I am just looking for a place where I can hang my hat and not be fucked around too much. Mexico is working out pretty good for me. And if that changes? I will be out of here like a bat out of hell.